# Empowering Employees

## Other titles in the Briefcase Series include:

A Briefcase Book

# Empowering Employees

### Kenneth L. Murrell
### Mimi Meredith

**McGraw-Hill**

New York  San Francisco  Washington, D.C.  Auckland  Bogotá
Caracas  Lisbon  London  Madrid  Mexico City  Milan
Montreal  New Delhi  San Juan  Singapore
Sydney  Tokyo  Toronto

# McGraw-Hill

*A Division of The **McGraw·Hill** Companies*

1 2 3 4 5 6 7 8 9 0 AGM/AGM   0 9 8 7 6 5 4 3 2 1 0

ISBN 0-07-135616-9

*This is a CWL Publishing Enterprises Book, developed and produced for McGraw-Hill by CWL Publishing Enterprises, John A. Woods, President. For more information, contact CWL Publishing Enterprises, 3010 Irvington Way, Madison, WI 53713-3414, www.cwlpub.com. Robert Magnan served as editor. For McGraw-Hill, the sponsoring editor is Catherine Schwent, and the publisher is Jeffrey Krames.*

*Printed and bound by Quebecor/Martinsburg.*

This publication is designed to provide accurate and authoritative information in regard to the subject matter covered. It is sold with the understanding that neither the author nor the publisher is engaged in rendering legal, accounting, or other professional service. If legal advice or other expert assistance is required, the services of a competent professional person should be sought.

> —*From a Declaration of Principles jointly adopted by a Committee of the American Bar Association and a Committee of Publishers*

McGraw-Hill books are available at special quantity discounts to use as premiums and sale promotions, or for use in corporate training programs. For more information, please write to the Director of Special Sales, McGraw-Hill, 2 Penn Plaza, New York, NY 10128. Or contact your local bookstore.

 This book is printed on recycled, acid-free paper containing a minimum of 50% recycled de-inked fiber.

# Contents

# Preface

During the final decade of the 20th century, *empowerment* became one of the most frequently used words in management. Unfortunately it also became one of the most misused concepts. Empowerment is not about making others more powerful; we really don't have that effect on others. Instead it is about making organizations both more effective and better places in which to spend major parts of our lives. It is about creating environments that promote high performance and high levels of appreciation among individuals.

With this book, we'd like to set the record straight. To inspire a deeper study of empowerment beyond the buzzwords. To show how you can bring the special quality of empowerment to your workplace. To illustrate that empowerment is not about managers losing power but about creating organizations in which everyone, including managers, gains power. To demonstrate how empowerment helps managers become even better leaders. To clarify that employees don't wait with bated breath to be empowered; they simply want to do a better job and enjoy their work in the process. To outline how managers and employees can grow on the job, become more knowledgeable and therefore more employable, and thus become fully empowered.

Together, then, everyone in the organization has something to gain by creating more empowering workplaces. Empowerment doesn't create narrowly focused gains for one individual or group; it does create far-reaching mutual gains for all.

Achieving those far-reaching—and long-lasting—gains is what this book is all about. We share with you the how-to of empowerment, and we expect you to share the techniques with others. We share with you some fictitious characters whose empowering experiences are based on real-life examples, and we expect you to apply what you learn from them. We share with you what we know empowerment *is* and what we know it *does*. We expect you and your organization to *be* empowering and to *do* empowering things that raise the bar even higher and set new standards for us who aspire to be empowered.

After all, empowerment is about mutual influence, shared knowledge, and the creation of power. We look forward to sharing them with you.

## Acknowledgments

Although we are grateful to a many people whose work or ideas motivated us, we are most grateful to our families. Ken's wife Cathy and children Kyra, Kenyan, and Jackson and Mimi's husband Max gave us their unquestioning and enthusiastic support throughout—and served as our inspiration on more than one occasion.

John Woods of CWL Publishing was helpful throughout the book's development, and we're thankful for his expertise. Robert Magnan, editor at CWL, did a fine job of editing the final manuscript.

Without Terry Armstrong, an extraordinary organizational development professional, this book might never have happened. Believing in the power of shared creativity and knowledge, Terry introduced Ken and Mimi, and for that we are in his debt.

Of course, we'd have had no reason to write this book at all were it not for those of you who work every day to improve your organizations and the lives of the people they affect. We hope that reading this book will speed you on your way to both personal and organizational empowerment.

## Special Features

The idea behind the books in the Briefcase Series is to give you
practical information written in a friendly person-to-person style.
The chapters are short, deal with tactical issues, and include
lots of examples. They also feature numerous boxes designed
to give you different types of specific information. Here's a
description of the boxes you'll find in this book.

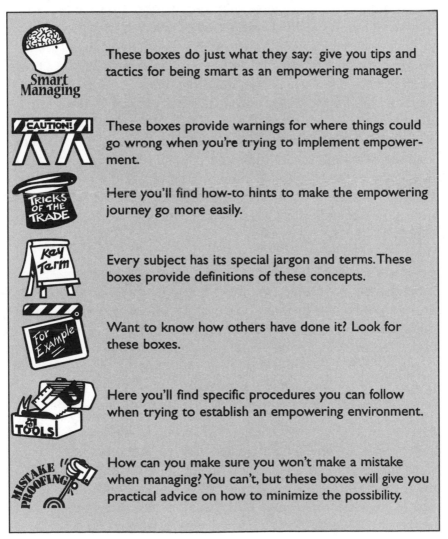

These boxes do just what they say: give you tips and
tactics for being smart as an empowering manager.

These boxes provide warnings for where things could
go wrong when you're trying to implement empowerment.

Here you'll find how-to hints to make the empowering
journey go more easily.

Every subject has its special jargon and terms. These
boxes provide definitions of these concepts.

Want to know how others have done it? Look for
these boxes.

Here you'll find specific procedures you can follow
when trying to establish an empowering environment.

How can you make sure you won't make a mistake
when managing? You can't, but these boxes will give you
practical advice on how to minimize the possibility.

## About the Authors

*Empowering Employees* is not **Ken Murrell**'s first brush with—
nor his first book about—empowerment. As professor of management and management information systems at the
University of West Florida, Pensacola, as an international consultant, and as a community activist, Ken has pioneered ways
of working and ways of thinking that build empowerment.

And that work has gained him recognition. He's worked with
the World Bank, the UN Development Program, the U.S. Agency
for International Development, and he's worked in Asia, Africa,
South America, and the Middle East. He's worked for small firms
and big ones like G.D. Searle, Motorola, Pfizer, BellSouth, and
Toyota. He's taught at American University in Cairo, at George
Washington and American Universities in Washington DC, at St.
Bonaventure, Columbia, DePaul, Brooklyn Polytechnic, Monterey
Institute of International Studies, University of Nebraska, Salford
University in the UK, Keil Centre in Scotland, and the University
of Miami. He currently is helping to develop new doctoral pro-
grams at Pepperdine in California and Benedictine University in
Illinois as well as a new master's degree program at Antioch in
downtown Chicago.

Recently, Ken chaired the board of the Academy of
Management's Organization Development and Change division,
and he is part of a growing group of Appreciative Inquiry practi-
tioners with the Taos Institute of New Mexico. Whatever the
task, Ken works with individual and organizational uniqueness
in mind. He prides himself on combining the theoretical and the
practical, and his passion is witnessing the ways in which
empowerment improves the quality of life in organizations.

**Mimi Meredith** owns Wordsmiths Unlimited, where for the last
seven years she has written, edited, and designed public relations
materials, training manuals, and books. She has a master's
degree in computer science, has been a social worker and a
trainer, and spent five years as a research associate at the
University of West Florida's Educational Research and

Development Center. In the late 1980s, she directed the development of Florida teacher certification tests in drama, speech, humanities, and journalism, and for teachers of the visually and physically impaired. She has taught business and professional communication, public speaking, and computer operating systems. Her community involvement has included PR and fundraising activities, particularly for Pensacola's Art Against AIDS.

An active member of the Society for Technical Communication, Mimi has conducted writing workshops for business, professional, government, and private enterprises. She has written for and edited the *Pensacola News Journal*'s magazine, *Business Today*. She's currently at work on a software manual, a humorous short story, and a collection of childhood remembrances for a product line of textiles, the result of a partnership with her three sisters.

# The Empowering Manager Is ...

Think about how you give meaning to a word. Take "manager," for example. A manager, by definition, is a leader, is an instructor, is a developer, is a coach, is a planner. So a manager is defined by what she or he *is*.

But a manager is also defined by what he or she *does*. A manager imparts knowledge or skill, shares the meaning of information, trains an employee to practice an occupation or profession, promotes learning by modeling certain behaviors, coaches employees toward understanding a system or structure.

So too we define the word "empowering" by what it *is* and by what it *does*. Empowering is mutual influence; it is the creative distribution of power; it is shared responsibility; it is vital and energetic, and it is inclusive, democratic, and long-lasting. Empowering enables people to use their talents and capabilities, fosters accomplishment, invests in learning, finds the spirit in an organization and builds effective relationships, informs, leads, coaches, serves, creates, and liberates. Becoming an empowering manager, therefore, involves both who you *are* and what you *do.*

While we're on the subject of words, why did we choose "empowering" over "empowerment" for the title of this book? For one significant reason. Because "empower*ment*" implies constancy—a state of being, a finished product, the end result of a process. "Empower*ing*," on the other hand, suggests action—enabling the growth of individuals and organizations as they add value to the products or services the organization delivers to its customers, and the promotion of continuous discovery and learning. For this reason, we've titled our book *Empowering Employees.*

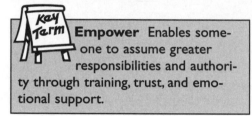

**Empower** Enables someone to assume greater responsibilities and authority through training, trust, and emotional support.

In an empowering organization, managers believe leadership derives from all its employees—not a select few. Managers of an empowering organization know that the company is most likely to succeed when employees have the tools, training, and authority to do their best work. Managers of an empowering organization understand that information is power—and they share it with all employees. Managers of an empowering organization value employees enough to build a culture that values and supports individuals. They want to make sure that everyone feels an ownership of that culture and a responsibility for its perpetuation. Managers of an empowering organization create opportunities for finding solutions and for designing what-can-be—not searching for problems and what-should-have-been. In an empowering organization, managers understand that fostering empowerment is a continuing effort—not an endpoint to be checked off a list of objectives.

**CAUTION!**

## Empowering is Not ...

If you carry an old map, you might miss the adventure of taking a new road. Try to mark these old roads—or ways of thinking—off your new, empowering map:

- Empowering is not proclaiming that you're emancipating the people who work for or around you.
- Empowering is not delegating all the work you don't want to do.
- Empowering is not something you do *to* or *for* someone else.
- Empowering is not making changes for the sake of change.
- Empowering is not creating teams so you can justify downsizing.
- Empowering is not leaving workers to fend for themselves.
- Empowering is not something that applies to "them" but not to "us."

## Empowering Is Mutual Influence

"When Tom, the new team leader for our assembly line, first suggested that we limit summer vacations to five days in order to meet our goals for the coming quarter, I was apprehensive," says Michelle, Tom's department manager. "I didn't think he'd considered things like union regulations, individual line workers' plans, and supply or inventory restraints.

"But what was I supposed to do?" Michelle continues. "I've been told that my new role as an empowering manager means that I shouldn't tell the team leaders what to do, that I should share responsibility with them, and that we should 'mutually influence' each other.

"When I let Tom go ahead with his plan, the reaction from the union reps and the line workers was swift—and negative. It's taken me weeks of negotiating and smoothing ruffled feathers to get us back on track. I know Tom feels like a failure, but I'm confused about what steps to take next. If he and I are equals, how can I give him the benefit of my experience without appearing to give him orders?"

Let's forget for the moment that Michelle pretty obviously hasn't received all the training she needs for her journey up the empowering highway. Instead, let's focus on her numerous—and valid—questions about what mutual influence is to an empowering manager.

In her pre-empowering life as a manager, Michelle understood her role completely. She answered to her boss for all the planning, scheduling, and implementing that went on in her department; her workers answered to her for their reactions to her actions. She understood influence, all right: she influenced the line workers by managing their work lives for them. Being influential was clearly a managerial role—and a big responsibility.

When Michelle's boss announced that the company's management had decided that it made sense to empower employees in order to respond to competitive pressures, she thought it sounded like a good idea. The word on empowerment was that it helped employees feel more motivated and be more productive. Instead of carrying all the weight for decision making on her own shoulders, she'd be able to relinquish some of her considerable responsibilities, and she'd help the people who reported to her develop their skills. She'd delegate power to her employees, and as they took on more responsibility and made decisions affecting their work, a good feeling would percolate through the group, and performance would improve as they worked more closely together in an empowering environment. However, this hasn't exactly happened. The question you might ask is *why*?

Michelle thought that there was some automatic mechanism that would kick in as soon as she began giving her employees more responsibility and authority. There'd be measurable improvement almost immediately—both in attitude and in productivity. She would learn it doesn't quite work like that.

It's clear that Michelle doesn't fully understand what empowerment is about and how it works. So let's explore the roots of Michelle's misunderstanding a little more.

First of all, we can think of empowering as a journey the organization is on. We all know that even a journey of a thousand miles begins with one step. You don't get to your destination without taking all the steps in between. The same is true in a metaphoric sense with regard to effectively creating an empowering and empowered work environment. But Michelle was trying her best to be what she understood an empowering manager should be—a non-invasive, laissez-faire kind of manager, whose employees would quickly rise to new performance levels, becoming self-directed and self-sufficient.

If Michelle had understood that an empowering environment is mutual influence and must evolve and grow as empowering experiences increase in the workplace, she'd have seen Tom's proposal in shades of gray instead of black and white. She'd have understood that together she and Tom could have learned from a discussion of what *both* of them knew about the proposed changes instead of *each* of them suffering a setback. Moreover, they might have avoided the problems they encountered by letting Tom go ahead with his idea with little discussion of its consequences. Had she understood that being mutually influential includes healthy, honest, nonjudgmental give-and-take, Michelle would have felt comfortable sharing her experience and questions with Tom—and she'd have gained insight into Tom's ways of thinking and working. She might also have discovered that Tom knew things she didn't and that Tom was capable of using what she did know in a way that would have resulted in a better plan for the line.

It might have helped Michelle to add "facilitator" to her definition of an empowering manager. She might then have understood her role to include

> **Key Term**
>
> **Facilitator** A person who removes obstacles and provides the support, information, feedback, and direction to help others succeed.

getting the right leadership to the right place, *not* failing to lead. And if Michelle had realized that participative planning is neither the easiest nor the fastest way for an organization to sort out its plans, she'd have allowed time for herself and Tom to practice working together. She'd have understood that mutual influence is the starting point for creating power.

## Empowering Is the Creative Distribution of Power

There's potential for a healthy balance, or *creative distribution*, of power in Michelle's and Tom's relationship—but they're definitely not there yet. Just how can they arrive at a creative

---

### Practicing Mutual Influence

What can you do initially to make sure your organization's goal of creating an empowering environment succeeds? Try taking these steps:

- Remember that empowering is a journey. Take one step at a time. Don't expect things to change overnight.
- Understand that mutual influence doesn't mean non-influence. It's more than OK to share your knowledge and experience as a manager; it's advisable. Mutual influence isn't either/or; it's both/together.
- Take time to listen, so you'll learn not only *what* but also *how* your employees think.
- Build honest, nonjudgmental give-and-take into manager–worker relationships. Doing so initiates respect, trust, understanding.

---

power distribution on their empowering journey? First, let's look at how we typically think of power. Isn't it usually a one-sided, one-person-over-another kind of concept? In our culture don't we most often think of power as being something that we must have and keep, something that we always must guard lest someone else wrest it from us? Isn't having power an issue of who's in control?

Traditionally, the answer to all those questions has been "yes." But we're not talking tradition here. We're talking evolution—*empowering* evolution. And that requires a change in the definition of power.

It might help to think about power from three perspectives (also see Figure 1-1):

- *Distribution:* Power is "given." This perspective implies that power is finite, that you lose power if you give it to someone else.
- *Creation:* Power is "made." This perspective implies that power is created when two or more individuals interact and share information, authority, and/or responsibility.
- *Creative distribution:* Power is "unlimited." This perspective implies that when people are mutually influential, power grows exponentially.

| View of Power | What I Do | What You Do | Total Value |
|---|---|---|---|
| Distribution (lose/win) | I give the power to you. Value: -1 | You take the power from me. Value: +1 | -1 +1 = 0 |
| Creation (win/win) | I share information with you. Value: +1 | You share information with me. Value: +1 | +1 +1 = 2 |
| Creative Distribution (win/win/share) | We influence each other and others. Value: >1 | We influence each other and others. Value: >1 | >1 +>1 = infinity |

Figure 1-1. The three evolutionary views of power

In an empowering organization, power becomes less about one person controlling another and more about the capacity within every person to create, develop, and distribute power to accomplish individual and shared goals.

Once we redefine power, we then can explore how power gets used in an empowering organization. Actually some pretty amazing things can happen. Instead of going it "alone at the top," managers find themselves buoyed by power that emanates from within *and* from without—from ideas, attitudes, and feelings of their own as well as from others. Instead of being burdened with the role of perpetual decision maker, the manager can be joined in leadership by others whose talents and skills are available when needed for a particular task. Instead of feeling that she or he must have all the answers all the time, the manager can be joined by others in a shared search for solutions. Instead of just ensuring that products get made and services provided, the

**Key Term**

**Power** Sometimes power is taken to mean the ability to exert force or to exercise authority, which implies that someone has control or advantage over someone else. When it comes to empowering organizations, however, power paints less the picture of individual might over individual might. It assumes more the vision that individual power + individual power > individual power x 2.

manager gains inspiration from the ideas of employees for how these products and services can be continuously improved.

Once Michelle understands mutual influence and redefines power, she's likely to feel more comfortable with her role and with Tom's. She's less likely to feel that their working relationship is all or nothing, total authority or none. She's more likely to realize that combining their ideas and creating power will produce a better result than either of them could produce alone.

You could liken an organization with an unhealthy distribution of power to an inexperienced sailor in rough seas. The boater stands at the helm with knees locked and body stiffened straight. When the boat rocks, the sailor rolls—constantly at odds with the boat, and feeling weaker every minute. The sailor feels the jolt of every wave, has a hard time keeping his or her footing, and aches for days afterward from the exhausting journey.

The empowering organization, one with a creative distribution of power, on the other hand, resembles the experienced sailor who rides rough seas with knees bent and body relaxed. When the boat rolls, this sailor rolls with it. This sailor's flexed knees cushion the blows from the waves, enabling her or him not only to maintain a balance but also to gain energy from the experience of dealing successfully with the rough sea. An organization like this welcomes competitive challenges, flexes according to fluctuating demands, and survives under any conditions—stormy or fair. Not surprisingly, organizations like this have loyal, involved, proactive crews.

One plus one no longer equals two. In an empowering organization, one plus one equals three or four or ten or.... Figure 1-2 illustrates how everyone wins—in ways that matter.

## Empowering Is Joint, Shared Responsibility

If individuals in a traditional organization were to do some brainstorming about what responsibility means, it might look like what's on Figure 1-3 (if you have some additional ideas, add them to the chart).

Before Michelle became an empowering manager (and we hope you know we use the term loosely here; the expectation

| Unhealthy Distribution of Power | Healthy, Creative Distribution of Power |
|---|---|
| Manager is hero or villain. | Manager is facilitator or coach. |
| Leadership is static; manager is always in control. | Leadership changes, depending on skills and talents required by the task at hand. |
| The workers and the manager expect the manager to have all the answers. | The workers and manager expect answers to be created together. |
| One individual has power over another; the amount of power in the organization is finite. | Individuals each add power to the power of others; the amount of power in the organization is infinite. |

Figure 1-2. The healthy and unhealthy distribution of power

that she "became" empowering overnight is, of course, totally unrealistic), how do you think she felt about responsibility? Probably, she envisioned responsibility something like what's printed on the flipchart in Figure 1-3. Probably she sometimes

**WHAT DOES RESPONSIBILITY MEAN?**
decision making
follow through
blame
credit
obligation
burden
duty
accountable
answerable
reliable
trust

_____

_____

_____

Figure 1-3. Brainstorming on the meaning of responsibility

found responsibility an unwanted burden. Probably she sometimes felt incapable of making a decision. Probably she sometimes felt blamed for things she couldn't control or credited with things she didn't deserve. Probably she sometimes felt obligated to shoulder responsibility, whether she felt up to it or not. But that's the role of a manager in a traditional organization. Whether it's the best way to accomplish goals, of course, is another issue. Our view is, and evidence bears this out, that it is not.

At other times, Michelle probably feels that responsibility is a good thing and that feeling trustworthy, reliable, and duty-bound makes each of us stronger and worthy of the credit we receive.

Still, as Michelle learns more about what an empowering organization is about and the value of the creative distribution of power, she's ready for the shift from lone to shared responsibility.

Why would she want to make that shift? For that matter, why would you? Let's look at some before and after illustrations.

**Before shared responsibility:** Decision making rests on the manager's shoulders. Credit and blame, deserved or not, arrive squarely at the manager's doorstep.

**After shared responsibility:** Decision making is shared with workers whose expertise fits the current need. Credit is celebrated and mistakes become opportunities for learning and improvement, not blame.

**Before shared responsibility:** Information "belongs" to the manager. The accountability buck stops here.

**After shared responsibility:** Information flows among all workers, including the manager. The accountability buck moves with it. Everyone understands that the best decisions and actions come when everyone has access to the information they need.

**Before shared responsibility:** The manager is burdened, weighed down by being the only person his or her boss deems trustworthy.

**After shared responsibility:** The load on the manager is lightened; the trust between manager and employees grows.

**Before shared responsibility:** The manager is forced always to be on the spot, available for trouble-shooting, ready with an answer at any time. (How can you take any time off under such circumstances?)

**After shared responsibility:** The manager is confident of the capabilities of the employees, available for consultation, a partner in finding answers.

OK, OK. This all sounds well and good. The picture's a pretty one. But how does anyone—Michelle, for example, or you—take the empowering journey to shared responsibility? Here's the route, in eight steps.

1. **Start small.** Choose one task in which to share responsibility, then choose an individual whose skills—combined with yours—match the demands of the task.
2. **Ensure understanding.** With the selected individual, discuss the task, the information needed to accomplish it, and the resources to be used.
3. **Decide who will do what and when.** Map the task, information, and resources—and the skills each of you brings to the task. If one thing must occur before another, agree on who (either or both of you) will make it happen and when.
4. **Write it down.** Put your "understandings" in writing, including the desired outcome (nothing lengthy, but clear and complete). Make a contract.
5. **Establish milestones.** Agree on times or events that will require each of you to make contact with the other, to guarantee that your task is on a steady course, not unnecessarily detoured.
6. **Don't be afraid to revise your plan.** As you share information and duties, you may make discoveries that give your project a new twist or that present new opportunities. Use your combined strengths to venture down some uncharted paths, if that seems appropriate or advantageous.

7. **Don't be afraid *not* to revise your plan.** If you can accomplish your task satisfactorily (albeit a little less inventively) without changing your original plan, and this shared responsibility stuff is still a little scary, stick with your original plan. You can be adventurous next time.

8. **When it's over, recap.** Once the task is complete, revisit what you did, why you did it, and how it turned out—not just the task itself, but your shared roles and responsibilities. Share with each other what you learned, what worked especially well, what you might change next time. Then, celebrate!

Why take all these steps? Maybe Michelle and Tom can illustrate it best.

To their credit, Tom and Michelle acknowledged that on their first steps on the empowering journey, they encountered some obstacles—but they didn't let these discourage them. They picked another task and used the eight-step process.

**Smart Managing**

**The Eight Steps to Shared Responsibility**
1. Start small.
2. Ensure understanding.
3. Decide who will do what and when.
4. Write it down.
5. Establish milestones.
6. Don't be afraid to revise your plan.
7. Don't be afraid *not* to revise your plan.
8. When it's over, recap—and celebrate!

The result was decidedly different this time. They completed their task easily, ahead of schedule, and they generated one new idea that would have a healthy impact on another task they want to try.

When they recapped the experience, they began to realize that some "un-tasklike" things had happened too. They knew much more about each other, who was good at one thing, who at another. They increased the quantity of information that flowed between them. They could easily account to each other—and anyone else who wanted to know—for just what they'd accomplished. Michelle and Tom were starting to feel more comfortable with the idea of an empowering organization and the changes it suggested for them. They didn't expect everything to go smoothly, but they had shared responsibility and were beginning to trust one another.

## Empowering Is Vital and Energetic

Thus far, we've described the act of empowering as starting small and growing, as being at first additive then exponential, as beginning with one or two individuals then spreading throughout an organization. Sounds like a pretty vital and energetic way to operate, don't you think? You'll want to know some ways to keep those levels up, won't you?

Here are some ideas for infusing yourself and your workplace with vitality and energy. First you lay the foundation for this empowering journey as you begin to create power and share responsibility. And then build on the foundation with actions like these:

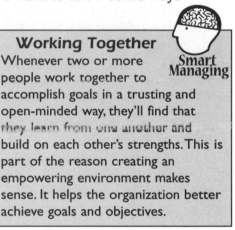

**Working Together**

**Smart Managing**

Whenever two or more people work together to accomplish goals in a trusting and open-minded way, they'll find that they learn from one another and build on each other's strengths. This is part of the reason creating an empowering environment makes sense. It helps the organization better achieve goals and objectives.

- **Encourage health.** Whether it's that your cafeteria serves fresh vegetables and fruits instead of canned, or that your budget allows for upgrading to more ergonomic equipment and furnishings, or that you encourage workers to move away from their computers for five minutes every hour, act in ways that show how you value health.
- **Promote community involvement.** A company that shares its time and talent with the community becomes more of a community itself—and a more satisfying place for valuable workers and managers to spend their time and talent.
- **Model a sense of humor.** We don't mean that you have to be a good joke-teller. We mean that laughter is good

**Keep 'Em Healthy**
A healthy workforce is a more productive workforce. And when employees understand that you care about their health, you enhance their commitment to the company and to their work.

for us all, physically and emotionally. So recognize that not all business is serious business, and employ humor to make yourself and those around you feel better.

- **Daydream a little—and allow it in others.** If you're constantly blinded by the headlights of today's crisis, you may never see the glow of a revolutionary idea. Give your mind a rest, and it's more likely to give you a fresh outlook.
- **Play a game every now and then**. Whether it's Scrabble in the break room, checkers on the lawn, or a vigorous game of basketball in the lot across the street, playing together means seeing a different side of the people you work with. You may discover hidden skills or knowledge. You may uncover qualities that a shy or boisterous facade otherwise masks.
- **Learn one new thing.** The new thing doesn't have to be intellectual or skillful or useful. You could learn to pronounce five words in the language of one of your customers, you could ask a coworker to teach you that new dance step he's been raving about, you could bone up on the history of a famous local resident. We're betting you'll want to learn one more new thing, and another, and ....
- **Introduce yourself to someone you pass in the hall every day but don't know**—someone outside your department or on another floor or in the next office suite. That person might just be someone who can give you advice, a new perspective, or maybe even change your worldview.
- **Break one old habit.** If you drive to work the same way every day, take a different route. If you return phone calls every day at 1:00, do it at 9:00 instead. Do one task differently; break out of that rut.

Taken together, activities like these energize you and those who work with you by making everyone feel better and think more clearly, expanding your knowledge, revitalizing your curiosity, extending the sphere of people who influence you. Be aware, though, that these actions may have unexpected side effects. You may find yourself devoting less time and energy to stress, conflict, and mind-deadening routine. But that's the idea.

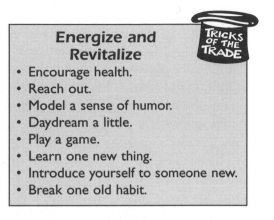

**Energize and Revitalize**
- Encourage health.
- Reach out.
- Model a sense of humor.
- Daydream a little.
- Play a game.
- Learn one new thing.
- Introduce yourself to someone new.
- Break one old habit.

## Empowering Is Inclusive, Democratic, and Long-Lasting

For 30 years now, one organization we know of has "reorganized" or "restructured" or "reengineered"—or just changed its name—with discouraging regularity. It has trained, retrained, and trained again, sometimes the same workforce, sometimes a new one. All this change has come from the top of the organization, the announcement of each change held captive until a legislative mandate or court order or piece of bad publicity forced its release.

Having once been part of this organization, we have little reason to hope that the next 30 years will be any better. But we're virtually certain they'll be worse, that is, if the organization is still around. The likelihood is it will not be.

We don't mean to say that there aren't good people in this organization, good support staff, good-communicating managers, good-hearted folks, good-thinking workers. We do mean to say that there are secrets in this organization, held by upper management but not by those who need the information. There's an entrenched hierarchy in this organization, with few channels of communication for sharing ideas with those at the top. Performance is rewarded by a change in title or a slight boost in pay; it's sometimes punished in the same ways.

So what can this organization do in the face of changing times except to superficially reorganize itself once again? It's what they've always done. Not having an awareness of the benefits of real change—the creation of an empowering culture—they have no way of knowing that an old map with a new name is still an old map. They have no way of realizing that their watchdogs and competitors are empowering themselves in a new century. They have no inkling that they may not survive beyond the beginning of the new century.

They're victims of the change-me/fix-me syndrome. A project falls on its face, a budget is cut, a department experiences massive resignations: they call a consultant, hire a change agent, bring in the latest, greatest training program. All in hopes that someone else will "fix" them. All efforts and saviors are doomed before they start.

Don't misunderstand: we're not knocking reorganization, the use of consultants, or training. We're knocking how they're misused.

When you hear "inclusive, democratic, long-lasting," what images do you conjure up? Probably not an organization like the one we've just described. Maybe we can get some ideas from revisiting Tom and Michelle.

**Change-me/fix-me syndrome** A wrong-headed approach to problem solving where managers make changes to supposedly solve problems without really understanding the true nature of the problem or what actions they can take to truly prevent such problems from occurring in the future. It is a quick-fix approach that never really fixes anything.

"I've been reading up on this 'empowering' stuff, Michelle," Tom says at the start of their next meeting. "Empowering organizations really aren't anything new. Some organizations were behaving in empowering ways long before someone coined the phrase. From what I can tell, empowering organizations—no matter whether they've been 'practicing' for decades or for weeks—are committed to including their workforces in decision making and planning. They continuously move toward more participation in envisioning the company's goals and reinforcing

> ## Change Isn't Always Good
> Change is a constant in our lives, and it's often a good thing. In fact, it's a vital part of an empowering journey. Change is usually not a good thing if it's done just for the sake of change, however. Don't fall victim to the change-me/fix-me syndrome. Empowering organizations realize that mutual influence, the creative distribution of power, shared responsibility, vitality and energy, and inclusive, democratic systems are critical to their survival, health, and growth. And all of these things take time to develop. So be suspicious of "overnight cures." They're tempting, but they just may lead you down an old road with a new name.

its ideals. And they end up being more productive for longer periods of time. Pretty impressive stuff."

Michelle thinks for a moment, then responds. "Remember that first 'empowering' experience we thought we had—where we both fell on our faces because we didn't really understand what empowering was? I thought we were supposed to change the way we operated overnight. Boy, was I off target! No wonder you didn't exactly trust my judgment. Now I'm beginning to realize that empowering is understanding where you're headed and why, it's accepting that it's a process, and it's based on solid values like the ones you just mentioned."

What can we learn from Michelle's and Tom's experiences? Here's one valuable lesson: If empowering is something you see as flipping a switch, changing your bottom line overnight, miraculously transforming your workforce into a participatory one just because you declare it so—well, you're bound for disappointment. And this is not to mention generating or reinforcing a lot of cynicism and distrust in workers who've already seen one too many flavor-of-the-month changes.

If, instead, you picture empowering as an ongoing process that ultimately includes all members of the organization and is founded less on the vision of one and more on the participation of many, you're more likely to produce longer-lasting results that are based on strong, unchanging values. And you'll be working with workers who can change their methods as necessary to meet the challenges of competition or expanding markets or new technology, because their values remain unchanged.

Now that we've confirmed what empowering *is*, we'll uncover what it *does* in Chapter 2.

## Manager's Checklist for Chapter 1

❏ Remember that an empowering organization sees achieving empowerment as a lifelong effort, not an endpoint to be checked off a list of objectives. Empowering an organization is an active journey, not a static destination.

❏ Recognize that empowering is not something you do to or for someone else, it is not making changes for the sake of change, and it is not something that applies to "them" and not to "us."

❏ Mutual influence, as practiced by an empowering manager, affects, supports, weighs, and impresses others—and accepts the same from them. The result? Shared information, knowledge, and feelings.

❏ A creative distribution of power reduces control, force, and advantage of one person over another. Instead, power is generated by and expands from each individual. When two people combine their power, the result is often greater than the sum.

❏ Shared responsibility boosts the flow of information, spreads accountability, and fosters partnerships that free managers from lone decision making and trouble-shooting.

❏ Infusing your workplace with vitality and energy—by modeling a sense of humor, encouraging health, introducing yourself to someone new, for example—reduces stress, conflict, and mind-deadening routine.

❏ Inclusion, democratic participation, and long-lasting effects strengthen empowering organizations. Such organizations rarely fall victim to the change-me/fix-me syndrome or flavor-of-the-month "cures."

# The Empowering
# Manager Does ...

*To be both a speaker of words and a doer of deeds.*
—Homer, *The Iliad*

It's Monday night. It's later than you'd like. You're more tired than you'd like. You can hardly put two thoughts together, except to wonder whether to plop fully clothed into your favorite chair, remote control and cold beer in hand, or to disrobe, slide into the tub, and close your eyes to the world.

Sometimes it's OK just to be—whether you're a couch potato or a tub lizard. Sometimes it's necessary to lie still, blinking occasionally to the rhythm of a TV sitcom or examining only the insides of your eyelids. But that's on Monday night–type occasions.

Tomorrow morning, you've got to do, don't you? Just as empowering *is* certain things—mutual influence, the creative distribution of power, shared responsibility, vital and energetic, inclusive, democratic, and long-lasting—empowering also *does* certain things.

**19**

While we're certain you'll discover some others along the way, the journey toward empowerment begins with doing things like these:

- Enabling talent and capability
- Fostering accomplishment
- Investing in learning
- Finding the spirit in an organization and building effective relationships
- Informing, leading, coaching, serving, creating, and liberating

So let's get started. We've go a lot of doing to do.

## Empowering Enables Talent and Capability

When last we saw Michelle and Tom, they had embarked on a new project and they were on their way to meet the guy with the "rep" in R&D. He's Arlo, the person they think holds the last piece to their new project's puzzle.

"Arlo," says Tom, "you've heard Michelle describe the challenges of our current project, and I've told you about the other team members. But we'd like to hear from you, now, about whether you'd be willing to join us and what you'd like to contribute."

Arlo looks at the floor, then looks at Michelle and Tom in turn. "First, I'm glad you two took the time to introduce yourselves and your project to me. It's something I think will benefit the company, and it's something that I think might have a role for me as it evolves.

"But I'm not sure I have the skills you expected. I'm not sure that I can help your team switch from the software they've been using to the one you plan to use."

Tom and Michelle share a disappointed glance.

"However, I'd suggest you get the entire team together and present the issue to them. That's what we did the last time our department faced a challenge—and it turned out that someone on our staff already had the skills we needed. We just hadn't known it before."

Having been part of an empowering group in his own department, Arlo had learned the value of uncovering talent within the organization. That's an important discovery.

What about you? Do you really know what talent exists in your team, department, or organization—or do you just think you know? When your project requires a particular skill, where do you look first—and how?

**Ability to Say No**

Working in an empowered environment means that employees also have the opportunity to turn down projects without jeopardizing future opportunities to take on additional responsibility. By respecting people and their assessment of their abilities to contribute, you help build a more motivated and dedicated group of employees who will respect you in return.

*Smart Managing*

If you run to human resources, start shifting your budget to accommodate a new contract employee, or write new and elaborate job descriptions for the perfect "fit," stop right there. If you haven't looked within first, start now.

Here's how Michelle and Tom did it. Let's attend the meeting they've called.

"We've asked you to this idea session," Michelle announces, "so we can help each other figure out how to make the transition from our old software system to the new one we've agreed we need for Project X." Michelle starts off a brainstorming session that includes the project team and Arlo.

"You'll recognize the chart we developed at our last session, where we itemized each skill and tool the project requires and where we agreed on responsibilities."

"Since we met last," Tom adds, "Michelle and I discovered that there was a gap. We realized that we hadn't planned for training on the new software—and it's a critical element of the project's success. Anyone have any suggestions?"

"Why don't we get on the Web and see if we can find a software consulting firm that can send in a trainer?" asks Marta, one of the line workers who's part of this team.

"Or see if there's someone in our own technology section

who can get free of their duties and help us get started?" suggests Lincoln, a hardware specialist on loan to the team.

"But are those options realistic?" interrupts Roberto, who keeps a tight rein on the project's budget. "There's not much chance of technology turning anyone loose. And won't finding and hiring a consultant take more time and money than we've allotted for this project?"No one answers for a moment. Denise, who's officially the team secretary, surveys her partners at the table, then says, "I should have mentioned this earlier, probably, but I didn't realize it was important. Before I left my last employer, I trained for several weeks on the new software we'll be using. And I trained my replacement. In fact, I think I still have the notes I created for her. I'd be glad to develop a series of training sessions with exercises that focus on the software features we'll use most. I don't think it will take long, since I'm so familiar with the content—and it's something I'd really enjoy doing. What do you think?"

What would *you* think? Denise's proposal offers expediency, knowledge, and enthusiasm—a winning combination. But do the Denises in your organization have the chance to make such proposals?

Talent and capability are easy to uncover if you know where and how to look. Let's examine what just took place for some clues.

First, Tom and Michelle expanded their horizons, so to speak, by approaching someone they didn't know in their organization. They then gave Arlo the information he needed to assess whether he'd be able to contribute to their efforts. When he realized he couldn't, they listened to his suggestion, decided it was valid, and laid it out for their team members. Last, they relied on the team's sense of shared responsibility for the project's outcome, and they trusted the team's ability to develop an effective plan of action.

Not only did the team members resolve the software training issue but they also created more power within. They'll be stronger individually and collectively—from learning to use a new tool and from relying on each other for creative problem solving.

### Enabling Talent and Capability

If your employees face a gap in skill or knowledge, try looking within the organization for help. You may be surprised at the resources you find there.

- Be sure to define the gap clearly. What is it you need in time, money, skill, knowledge, equipment, materials?
- Before you head outside the company for talent, consult the talent inside. You'll practice brainstorming alternatives, share decision-making, and increase knowledge.
- Don't limit yourself to the team or department. Open yourself up to the organization as a whole. (And maybe you'll have a chance to meet someone you've not known before—someone who represents an untapped resource.)
- If you can't find what you need within the organization, don't hesitate to look for talent and capability outside—just be sure you've sought the input of those inside the organization whose work will be affected by this choice.
- Once you find the talent you need, create a contract that clearly states what's expected from everyone involved.

This is not to say that you'll never need an outside consultant, that you'll never again need to hire a new person to fill a gap in skill, or that every volunteer will produce the results you need. Our point here is that empowering managers enable the application of talent and capabilities that exist within their organizations. Perhaps taking Arlo's advice is the best evidence so far that Michelle and Tom are definitely on the road to empowerment.

There's little doubt that, while helping to build the team's power, Denise was empowered as an individual. The more she contributes, the more she finds pleasure in her job, the more she'll add value to this project—and the next.

## Empowering Fosters Accomplishment

Let's assume that Denise successfully designs and delivers the software training program. (This story is based on a true one, by the way, and the "real" Denise succeeded beyond anyone's expectations.) Just how is it that an empowering organization fosters such accomplishment?

**Built to Last**

Sometimes organizations with characteristics like we're describing in this book are thought of as "built to last." This term comes from a best-selling book of the same title that examined some of the traits of our most admired and successful companies. In their book *Built to Last*, James C. Collins and Jerry I. Porras identify exceptional companies that have "stood the test of time" and uncover what makes them different from other companies. Here are just a few of those revelations:

• Companies that are built to last are admired by other companies.
• Companies that are built to last have an impact in their communities.
• Companies that are built to last succeed over time, through successions in leadership, and despite changes in products.
• Companies that are built to last have a core ideology, a belief system that remains constant.

You know how Tom, Michelle, and Arlo fostered Denise's accomplishment. What about the larger organization? What characterizes an organization that's empowering?

One thing that empowering, built-to-last organizations have in common is that they foster accomplishment in individual employees, in groups, and in the organization as a whole. They don't require a lone, powerfully charismatic leader; they don't exist solely to corner a market or only to make their shareholders wealthy.

Do these characteristics remind you of anything? Does it sound suspiciously as though built-to-last companies promote creative distribution of power, shared responsibility, vitality, and inclusive, long-lasting vision—just as empowering organizations do? If so, your intuition is correct.

Managers who act in ways that enhance empowerment, then, also foster long-term accomplishment and contribute to building organizations that endure. Employees who are party to an organization's purpose often volunteer their skills, as Denise did, so they feel a sense of contribution to the organization's accomplishment.

Ultimately, empowering managers understand how power—that infinite resource—is created and they understand that its creation makes each employee more powerful, makes the manager more powerful, makes the organization more powerful—and fosters accomplishment. What a way to work!

## Empowering Invests in Learning

What comes to mind when you think of "investment"? Deposits to your retirement account? Quarterly reports on your mutual funds' earnings? Savings for your child's education? Buying a piece of property you think will appreciate?

### Motorola's Key Beliefs

At Motorola, enabling talent and capability is supported by the company's "key beliefs": constant respect for people and uncompromising integrity.

Although the company may do lots of things differently in the future, these beliefs are one thing that won't change, according to Chris Galvin, Motorola's third-generation CEO.

With each investment, you receive returns of some sort: increased security for your old age, heightened value for the bottom line on your financial statement, insurance that your child will be equipped for adulthood, an extra source of funds for the inevitable rainy day.

Do you think of going to work each day as an investment? Empowering managers do. Why? Let's reconsider Denise's training program from the viewpoint of a prospective investor.

Investing in the software learning program required Michelle and Tom to define their needs, seek help outside their team, and then work within the team. In other words, they devoted time and analytical skills to their investment. Investing in Denise's ability to deliver the program required that Tom and Michelle trust in someone else's talent and capability. Investing in the team's decision-making ability meant that Michelle and Tom understood how the returns of that investment would be higher productivity and a team that effectively contributes to achieving organizational goals.

Not much different from any other investment, wouldn't you say? The nature of the investment may be different, but the results are the same. As an empowering manager, your investment in learning for yourself and your employees pays off, in the short run and in the long. That payoff doesn't just redistribute existing resources; it creates new ones.

But let's put a real-life face on investing in learning. Let's look at the Japanese business philosophy of *kaizen* or continuous improvement. While American companies often are renowned for startling innovation, Japanese companies often want to be known for their capacity for ongoing improvement.

And why not? Constant, gradual, steady, small improvements by the Japanese, in the quality of both processes and products, resulted in the "miracle" of their economic recovery after World War II. Had they been satisfied with an initial success and adopted an if-it-ain't-broke-don't-fix-it philosophy, the miracle might never have occurred. Had they opted for an I-don't-care-how-you-do-it-just-do-it philosophy, a results-oriented one, the miracle might never have occurred. Had they settled for a control-quality-at-the-end-product way of thinking, instead of building quality into each process and each product, the miracle surely never would have occurred.

> **Key Term**
>
> **Kaizen**  This Japanese term means *continuous improvement* in every aspect of one's life, at home, in society, and on the job. It means never being satisfied and continually identifying small ways to make things better. Over time, this results in dramatic improvements in quality, reductions in cost, and increased satisfaction by all involved.

The *kaizen* approach is mirrored in what we've witnessed about Tom and Michelle thus far. With each step they take in their journey toward empowerment, they learn from the preceding step and expand that learning to the next step. The result? A continuous, ongoing spiral of improvement.

So Michelle and Tom, perhaps without realizing it, invested in their team's learning in more ways than one. They invested in Denise's learning from her previous experience. They also invested in the team's learning a new skill (using the new software), and they invested in the organization's learning about an empowering process: the ability to learn from an event or experience and to continuously build on it, adding value to people and products along the way.

You could compare such an experience to doing research for a marketing plan, for example. You begin with the seed of an idea, which inspires you to read related trade and professional publications, which give you new ideas, which help germinate the seed, which grows and fills your mind with new seedlings of ideas, which you read up on in publications, which give you more new ideas. ... Well, you get

**Toyota's Investment in Learning**

An assistant manager at Toyota compared an auto part whose design doesn't get updated to a piece of fruit that doesn't get refrigerated: they're both rotten. As part of a system that thrives on constant improvement, Toyota's employees have a long history of making suggestions that stop the company's fruits from rotting—and that contribute to individual and corporate learning, whether from mistakes, serendipity, or flashes of genius. New ideas can come from anyone, anywhere. Investing in learning reaps continuous improvement. (For more, read *Kaizen: The Key to Japan's Competitive Success*, by Masaaki Imai.)

the picture. Before you know it, you're the author of a creative, credible—perhaps incredible—marketing plan, or a new R&D discovery, or an improved manufacturing process. Improvements just keep on coming.

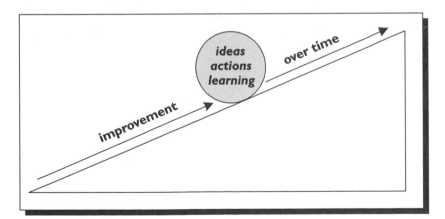

Figure 2-1. The movement toward ever higher levels of improvement and performance from Kaizen

**Smart Managing**

### Apply a Kaizen Approach

Consider learning an invest-ment—and act on it. Even if you think you already know the answers, don't make assumptions. Find out what ideas your employees have and capture those ideas, whether casually in a one-on-one hallway conversation, more inclusively in a group meeting, or more formally in a written suggestion system. Then share those ideas so that others can build and act on them, so that more improvement ideas will be generated, so that customers will be more satis-fied, and on and on. If you feel a little dizzy at first, just relax and realize that even if improvement slows down at times it will never cease. That's the return from investing in learning.

In Japan, the *kaizen* approach is essential not only to the workplace but also to the family and to social institutions. It applies not only to employees but also to managers and CEOs. It is part of an orga-nization's spirit.

## Empowering Finds the Spirit and Builds Effective Relationships

The spirit of your organi-zation encompasses its mission and its vision—not necessarily the ones that are posted in the hallways, but the ones that are evi-denced by its behaviors. The spirit of your organization derives from its ways of doing—whether it's developing policies, design-ing products, or defining services. And the spirit of your organi-zation derives from its ways of interacting—with its employees, with its suppliers, and with its customers.

Where does your organization's spirit come from? Why is it important? Spirit comes from being able to answer these ques-tions: "Who are we?" "What do we believe?" "Why are we here?" Spirit is important because it embodies your organiza-tion's core values and separates built-to-last companies from less resilient ones.

### Core Values

We recently heard a consultant colleague remark, "If they can't tell me who they are, I won't work with them." Harsh words? Maybe not. Her point was that she could design dynamite advertising campaigns, produce bang-up public relations pieces, and attract new customers en masse. She could re-create their company in any image they wanted. She could boost their name recognition off the charts. She could send their sales prospects over the top.

> **Spirit** We're talking about the spirit of an organization, not a new religion. Spirit in this context is an aliveness created by the presence of a shared vision and a heartfelt commitment to something bigger than oneself.

But she couldn't improve their bottom line unless they could answer the question "Who are we?"

Why? Because if the external picture she created for all those new customers didn't match the picture they saw once they were inside the company's door, all her efforts were for naught. If the advertising campaign was based on some wannabe image of the company and not on its firmly held beliefs, the campaign would produce lots of prospects but few purchases. If the public relations efforts were based on pie-in-the-sky instead of deeply ingrained values, the words were wasted.

So, if a company can't tell her who they are, she says good-bye—unless or until they can identify the company's core values.

A recent experience illustrates further the need to articulate your company's core values. One of us wanted to explore options for a new cellular phone. An out-of-town friend had mentioned the "deal" he'd gotten with a particular provider, one whose ads we'd seen and who was well known nationwide, so we went to the yellow pages in search of a local representative. What we found was no local listing but a toll-free number, which we dialed.

A recorded message answered. We punched in the number that corresponded to "information" and waited. And waited. And never got an answer.

No slouches in the electronic communications arena, we searched the World Wide Web, knowing

> **Core values** If you look in the dictionary under "core," you'll find words like "innermost," "central," and "essential." For "values," you'll find "concepts of what's worthwhile" or "principles." Core values, then, are the principles that are essential to your company's worth—and what it believes and how people interact to get work done.

this household-word company would have a Web site. Sure enough, they did, and we went there.

They asked for our ZIP code so they could provide us with a local contact. We typed it in. They replied that there was no company representative in our area.

Impossible, we thought. So we searched the Web site for their reps in our state. Sure enough, there was one right in our hometown and—hooray!—there was a local phone number.

We signed off the Web site and dialed the number. The party who answered announced the name of a local educational institution: wrong number. We apologized, went back to the Web site, verified the phone listing, and redialed—and got the same educational institution. Seething, we pounded our way back to the Web site, fired off an email about the invalid phone number, and received a thank-you email ... two days later.

Would you buy a cell phone and service from this company? One that touts its expertise and reputation as a communications standout, yet acts in ways that communicate just the opposite— that it's totally out of touch?

Like our consultant colleague, we don't even want to begin a relationship with this organization. If there are any core values at work here, we can't tell it. When you come right down to it, core values are at the heart of building relationships, both internal and external to your team, department, company, or community. If the values aren't there, neither are long-lasting relationships.

Core values don't change with the wind or with the stock market. They don't have to be reevaluated, revised, or rewritten. By their very nature, they are the soul of your organization. Without them, you're less than likely to present a consistent, responsive, recognizable face to the ever-changing world. With them, you can confidently change your strategies, your plans, or your market, while retaining the essence of your company that people will grow to trust. If you can't find the spirit in your organization, then start by finding the core values. Ask, "Who are we?" "What do we believe?" "Why are we here?" Answering these questions will move you up the empowering road toward building

---

### How to Know a Core Value if You See One

Core values come in many forms. They may be based on a 100-year-old statement from the company's founder, they may have been articulated by committee, or they may have been inspired by a lone employee. Nevertheless, they all represent your company uniquely—they're not borrowed from someone else's idea of value. Here are some examples.

- Honesty above profit.
- Adaptability to changing customer needs.
- Respect for all members of the organization.
- Appreciation of mistakes as learning opportunities.

---

honest relationships with your employees, your suppliers, and your customers alike—and it will build in resiliency.

### Trust

Although the electronic age promised us more leisure, it seems to have delivered less. Timesaving devices seem to result in time spending. Having information at our fingertips has evolved into information overload.

All the more reason to be grounded in a set of core values that support relationships—relationships that support individuals in finding an effective balance between work and play. If you want to support relationships, you'll need to invest in a little trust.

Michelle and Tom continuously check their mile markers on their road to empowerment. Today they're talking about trust.

"I'm just not sure that Sarah's ready to hear about Denise's software training program," Tom frowns, talking to Michelle about their Director of Training and Development. "She's given it lip service, but she still hasn't bought into the idea of participation and fostering talent at whatever level it appears in the organization. I'm just worried that she'll sabotage Denise's success."

"But we can't *not* tell her," Michelle replies. "For one thing, she's the training expert; for another, Denise could be a valuable resource for other departments who may want to change over to the new software. No way would Sarah have time to conduct all that training alone."

**Smart Managing**

### Building Relationships with Trust

If you want to be an empowering manager, you'll need to infuse your relationships with trust. As Ken Murrell and Judith Vogt observed, "Those who are not trusted consume inordinate amounts of time and energy in terms of managerial efforts to control them. Whatever they produce has been cajoled from them, at great cost, in a zero-sum exchange: their contribution minus the manager's efforts."
("The Manager as Leader in an Empowering Organization: Opportunities and Challenges," in *The 1991 Annual Handbook: Developing Human Resources,* La Jolla, CA: University Associates.)

"How can we do it in a way that doesn't threaten Sarah, then," Tom asks, "and doesn't jeopardize Denise's efforts?"

"I'm a big fan of lists. Why don't we list pros and cons for Sarah? What would be good for her if she supported Denise's training program and what would be bad? That way, I think she'll appreciate our honesty and maybe she'll be more receptive because of it. Even if she's not, we can at least say we were trustworthy."

Just what are Michelle and Tom doing? They're building their relationship with Sarah and they're building it on trust. They're not trying to pull any wool over Sarah's eyes. They're giving her the facts, and the odds are that she'll remember that.

In Treasury Secretary Alan Greenspan's commencement address to Harvard University's Class of '99,* he pointed out that economic systems based on mutual benefit have trust at their core; without it, he says, "no economy can prosper." Success, Greenspan is certain, depends on your integrity and character and on how principled you are. "Of even greater import is that all Americans believe that they are part of a system they perceive as fair and worthy of support." There's nothing about increasing the bottom line, nor commanding more market share, nor changing the balance of imports to exports. It's just integrity, principles, and trust.

If your employees are like most, they increasingly want more from their companies than simply a place to go to work. They want work relationships that matter and they want organizations in whose beliefs they can trust. If you take one step at a time

*Alan Greenspan, "Transcending All Else Is Being Principled," *The Harvard University Gazette,* June 17, 1999.

toward trust, as Michelle and Tom did, you'll build relationships. And you and your workforce will gain value—and continue to improve. *Kaizen!*

## Empowering Informs, Leads, Coaches, Serves, Creates, and Liberates

Now you know what empowering does: enables talent and capability, fosters accomplishment, invests in learning, finds the spirit, and builds relationships. But what can *you* be and do that will heighten your empowering skills? Well, that's what you'll find in the chapters that follow.

Conceptually, we start with the assumption that all managers must be skilled in six areas: informing, decision-making, evaluating, motivating, planning, and developing.

We then move to the "first generation" of ways of empowering that act on those assumptions: educating, leading and following, organizing and structuring, mentoring and supporting, providing and resourcing, and actualizing and realizing.

Finally, we look at "second generation," or enhanced empowering competencies as in Fig 2-2: learning for self, team, and organization; transforming with shared responsibility; liberating existing structures; coaching and counseling; serving through sustainable systems; and creating continuous quality.

Empowering managers are adept in all six different areas, or competencies, and you'll learn them all.

In this chapter and in Chapter 1, we've focused on empowering, on what it *is* and what it *does*, trying to give you just an inkling of what's to come.

Chapters 3 through 8 will review each of the six core competencies of empowering managers: informing, leading, coaching, serving, creating, and liberating. Chapter 3, Getting to Knowledge, asks, "Are you in the know?" and examines the route of meaningful information, where it comes from and where it flows. You'll learn to clarify the language of your organization, to develop a practical model for sharing knowledge, and to appreciate the benefits of the informing–educating–learning triad.

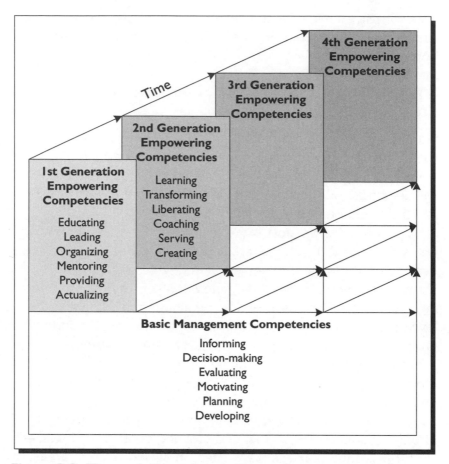

Figure 2-2. The evolution of competency for an empowering manager

If you want to understand the symbiotic relationship between empowering and leading—and if you want to develop your own leadership skills—Chapter 4 will help you know when and how to lead and when to follow.

Chapters 5 and 6 evaluate Who's at Work Here? and What's at Work Here? from taking good care of yourself to re-energizing your workforce with the three R's of empowerment: respect, resources, and reinvestment.

Tired of retooling, reinventing, reengineering? Learn to make more with what you've got in Chapter 7. In Chapter 8,

Empowering the Workforce, you'll unlock the secrets of what makes people love—or hate—their jobs, and what you can do about it. And you'll walk away with liberating, motivating strategies.

In the last two chapters, you'll cruise toward an empowering future with forward-looking approaches. Learn about benchmarking high performance and about promoting it—all in Chapter 9, Ask the Right Questions. Learn the unique rewards of the appreciative inquiry approach and gain new insights into performance evaluation.

When you're a manager, "challenge" is an oft-heard buzzword—and it sometimes even feels like your middle name. Chapter 10, Empowering for the Future, both challenges you and helps you address technology, privacy, ethics, core values, and philanthropy—and create a long-lasting, empowering environment.

In the Appendix, you're the focus: Which of your characteristics are more empowering? Which are less so? What behaviors of yours move you toward empowerment? Which do not? In a survey of your management style, you'll acquire self-knowledge and you'll gain direction toward empowerment.

Ultimately, challenges require you to make choices. You'll have choices aplenty to make on the road to becoming an empowering manager. With this book, you'll have a roadmap to empowering management.

## Manager's Checklist for Chapter 2

❑ Look for talent and capability within your organization first. You'll discover things you never knew about the people you work with—and you may save time and money, too.

❑ If you want to become more empowering and be part of a company that's built to last, you must foster accomplishment by creating opportunity for employees to break through their traditional assumptions about work and their responsibilities and opportunities.

❏ Investing in learning is a lot like investing in a climbing stock market. Working with employees to improve their performance is another kind of investment that reaps high returns in productivity and job satisfaction. Adopt the *kaizen* approach of continuous improvement.

❏ If you don't know already, find your organization's core values. If you do know, spread the word. You can always change a policy, but you should never have to change your values.

❏ Remember the six basic assumptions about what managers must do: inform, make decisions, evaluate, motivate, plan, and develop—and read on to start your evolution!

# Getting to Knowledge: The Route to Meaningful Information

*A wise man has no extensive knowledge;*
*He who has extensive knowledge is not a wise man.*
*The sage does not accumulate for himself.*
*The more he uses for others, the more he has himself.*
*The more he gives to others, the more he possesses of his own.*
*The Way of Heaven is to benefit others and not to injure.*
*The Way of the sage is to act but not to compete.*
*—Lao-tzu, The Way of Lao-tzu*

"That's what I get for taking a few days off! I return from a long weekend vacation, only to find 214 emails waiting. How on earth am I going to catch up?"

"Six trade magazines are sitting on my desk right now. I have no idea how I'll find time to read them. Before I know it, six more will be added to the stack."

"Yesterday, a client asked me about a new product she'd seen on the Internet. She wondered whether I thought she should use it. What could I say? No way I can keep up with all the information that's 'out there' now!"

You probably hear comments like these almost every day—in fact, you probably make them yourself. With all the information that's "out there" now, do you know anyone who can keep up or who doesn't get frustrated trying? And just what do you get when you do manage to access the information in the great "out there"? Data? Knowledge? Wisdom?

---

**Smart Managing**

### The 80/20 Principle

"The 80/20 Principle asserts that a minority of causes, inputs, or effort usually lead to a majority of the results, outputs, or rewards. Taken literally, this means that, for example, 80 percent of what you achieve in your job comes from 20 percent of the time spent."

Taken further, this means that perhaps 80% of the information you find valuable comes from 20% of the information you take in. If you begin to identify that valued 20%, you'll decrease the amount of information you must deal with and free up some of the time you spent on that overvalued 80%.

(Richard Koch, *The 80/20 Principle: The Secret of Achieving More with Less*, New York: Currency/Doubleday, 1998, p. 4).

---

If you're very lucky, you may acquire some of each—but that's rare. More often than not, most of us don't have time to make sense of the information that beats a path to our door every day. We're fortunate if we even get to open the door, much less gain some kind of knowledge from what enters.

What's an empowering manager to do? Who has time to be empowering *and* knowledgeable? The answers lie in the first building block of empowerment: understanding why information is important, where it comes from and where it goes, and what you can do to transform it into knowledge and wisdom, both individual and organizational.

## Are You in the Know?

Just what is it that makes so much information seem so important? Use the examples we've supplied in Figure 3-1 to start an internal dialogue about how information, or the lack thereof, affects you. Jot down on a sheet of paper your own observations.

| Without information, I must ... | With information, I can ... |
| --- | --- |
| • Stick with what I know<br>• Limit myself to what"s "given" in my area of expertise<br>• Replay existing ideas over and over again<br>• Pretend to have all the ideas I need | • Discover new ideas in my field<br>• Find out what goes on in areas outside my field<br>• Generate new ideas based on new—or newly considered—information<br>• Share the power of ideas within my group or organization |

Figure 3-1. With and without information

Notice the words that begin the "Without information" column: *stick, limit, replay, pretend.* And the ones that begin the "With information" column: *discover, find, generate, share.* Which verbs would you rather use to characterize your own actions? We suspect you'd prefer the "With" column.

Now, think about ways in which information—or the lack of it—affects you and your workforce every day. Use the flipchart in Figure 3-2 to list two types of information: what you have too much of and what you don't have enough of. (Again, we've inserted a few examples to get you started.) We'll come back to this chart at

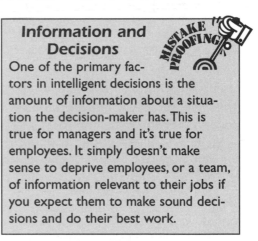

**Information and Decisions**

One of the primary factors in intelligent decisions is the amount of information about a situation the decision-maker has. This is true for managers and it's true for employees. It simply doesn't make sense to deprive employees, or a team, of information relevant to their jobs if you expect them to make sound decisions and do their best work.

the end of the chapter, to see whether what you've learned will help you manage information in empowering ways.

Now that you've listed some of your own information needs and gaps, let's look in on Michelle and Tom. They're back, but they're not talking entirely about work—yet.

"Yesterday, Tom, I read a headline in the local paper that struck pretty close to home: 'People's ideas sought for work on

| Too Much Information | Too Little Information |
|---|---|
| • about latest trends in management | • about what works for managers |
| • on the newest versions of software | • on how to use software to my advantage |
| _____ | _____ |
| _____ | _____ |
| _____ | _____ |
| _____ | _____ |
| _____ | _____ |
| _____ | _____ |

Figure 3-2. Information brainstorm: Too much and too little

Jackson Avenue,'" Michelle says. "Since Jackson is that heavily traveled, grossly congested feeder street that connects my 'bedroom community' to the rest of the world, I took a couple of hours' leave to attend the meeting.

"The county engineer began by sharing information he has: one particular section of road seems to cause the most problems, there are options for widening it or adding more turn lanes, and there are projected increases in daily traffic. Then the road contractor tells us that plans for three phases of work have been developed already—but, he says, 'I want to hear from those of you who travel the road every day. We've studied the situation for a couple of weeks, but you've lived with it for years. We need your input.'

"Well," Michelle goes on, "I'm pretty impressed already. I've never had anyone ask what I know *before* they start work on a project like this.

"The first member of the public to speak shows the group a journal he's kept during two years' worth of commuting. He'd actually documented how much time he spends each morning in the existing turn lane, from the time he must first stop his car until the time he actually turns right onto the highway.

"Next, a young mother goes to the podium. Two of her kids attend the school that borders the 'problem area.' She tells us that although the traffic bottleneck is a problem, her biggest concern is the need for sidewalks and protected crossings for her kids.

"To make a long story short, before the meeting ends, the three-stage plans were redrawn to include sidewalks, the commuter's journal convinces the engineer to add a second right-turn lane, and I find myself volunteering to talk to the school board about establishing guarded crosswalks."

Tom smiles and says, "Boy, sounds like you got your money's worth for those few hours off. The experience really got you excited, didn't it?"

What created such excitement for Michelle? The same kinds of things that can create excitement in your workplace: asking for information and sharing facts, input, data, and actions that result in each individual knowing more, in the group acting more effectively, and in the organization or community benefiting in unanticipated ways.

> **Shared Information, Shared Commitment** Smart Managing
> When people confront a problem together, share their various perspectives on solutions, gather information from one another and then agree to take action, this greatly enhances their commitment to following through. Why? Because (1) they've been listened to and trusted with the same information as everyone else, (2) they won't want to let the group down, and (3) the solution is theirs.

So what gives information value? What makes information important?

First, information becomes important because of its source—for example, the data kept in the commuter's journal or the feelings expressed by the concerned parent. The information they supplied was genuine, timely, accurate, and honest, regardless of whether it took the form of fact or feeling.

Second, information becomes important because of the way it's processed. In our example, the county engineer and the road contractor considered several sources as objectively as they could: highway department data, commuter and parental input, and existing construction plans. But they didn't stop there: they wondered aloud about the effects of differing approaches before the plans were finalized. By doing so, they let the other participants witness their thought processes and, along with those participants, they grew more powerful and more knowledgeable.

Last, information becomes important because of the way in which it is applied. Because all the individuals at the meeting gained knowledge about the project, their output was far stronger and their solutions far longer-lasting than if decisions had been made in isolation or with less information.

Being in the know doesn't have to mean being swamped with information. In the rest of this chapter, you'll learn more about discovering, finding, generating, and sharing information, knowledge, and wisdom in empowering ways—for yourself, and for and with others.

---

**Being in the Know**

**TOOLS** If you want to turn information into advantage, put these tools to work.

- Eliminate guesswork. Ask for information; don't wait for it to come to you.
- Rely on data from sources you trust.
- When in doubt, seek an alternative point of view.
- Insist on accuracy, relevance, and timeliness.
- Capture information for the record; it may be more useful than you know in the future.
- Consider the value of both facts *and* feelings.

---

## Where Does Knowledge Come From?

For empowering managers, being in the know requires more than just collecting information. In order to understand where knowledge comes from, perhaps we'd better start with what it is—and that means we need to define "information," "knowledge," and "wisdom."

*Information* is all about facts, data, and input from others about particular situations. It's valuable because it allows you to make comparisons among facts and data to better understand situations. *Knowledge* is know-how. Knowledge comes from experience and training and is enhanced by information because it helps you improve your ability to accomplish tasks. *Wisdom* is not just know-how but knowing what actions are right, moral, and just as you confront various situations. Wisdom comes more often from insight than from facts or knowledge. It comes with experience, effort, and reflection.

So (going back to our "empowering is ..." premise from Chapter 1) an empowering manager *is* informed, knowledgeable, and wise—and helps others become so. Why? Because it improves the quality of everyone's performance, including the manager.

> **The Wisdom of Empowering**
>
> One trait of a wise manager, one who understands what's right and just, as well as sensible, is that he or she intuitively seeks to empower employees. This is wise because it brings out the best in those employees and their manager.

### Inform–Educate–Learn

There's another triad we need to address: informing–educating–learning. This is where the "empowering does ..." part from Chapter 2 meets your management style. (We'll get around to assessing that style in the Appendix.) If you want to progress from basic skills to first- or second-generation empowering management, you inform, educate, and learn. But how?

By recognizing that, ultimately, the importance and value of information comes down to the people who provide it and the ways in which they share it. In Michelle's experience, for example, the local government sought the public's ideas because drivers usually know the problem spots best. What does this say about the information you solicit or don't solicit from your employees, from members of other organizations, from your customers? It says that the source of all information is *people* and that you'll increase the value of people, information, and products by:

- *informing* employees in a timely manner of the information they need using means such as information systems to make sure it's available when and where they need it. This is one step in building a foundation of trust.
- *educating* employees, which is a first-generation empowerment skill, you help them develop their skills, better understand the big picture of the organization, and demonstrate the importance of continued learning for everyone so they can be more effective contributors to the organization.
- encouraging real *learning*, which is a second-generation empowering skill, you promote high performance and continuous improvement. You help employees understand that learning involves not just a few hours of classroom time; it is a full-time activity and opportunity. You help your employees understand that knowledge and wisdom give you, your employees, and the whole organization competitive advantage and unlimited growth potential.

What happens while you're *doing* all these informing, educating, and learning kinds of things? Besides helping your employees, you enhance your own skills. It is a basic truth that those who teach and train others become more skilled themselves.

## Unlearn

There's something else you begin to realize about information, as you create an empowering environment. You realize that *un*learning is also necessary—and may be the greatest challenge to becoming an empowering manager. Let's consider *un*learning for a moment. While you're preoccupied with the constant need to learn more, don't forget to erase some of these old tapes:

- *Unlearn the idea that you must read every email or review every journal, newsletter, or magazine that comes across your desk.* Make use of the technology that's available to you to screen or filter your email, sorting it into categories so you can narrow your "must-read" list.

Read only the introduction and/or the conclusions of a journal article; then, go back and read the entire article if it's relevant. (And if you haven't read a trade publication for six months or more, cancel your subscription! At least, you'll eliminate the guilt you feel watching the issues pile up on your desk. At best, you'll make room for a publication that you *will* read.)

- *Unlearn the concept that technology is an answer in itself, that having more or better equipment will solve all your information problems.* Remember that the source of all information is ultimately the people behind it. How many times have you read about a school or a business installing state-of-the-art equipment, only to have it sit idle (often because no one's been trained to use it) until it's obsolete? Consider first what upgraded technology will do for the people who create, process, and apply information before you decide that a piece of hardware or software is "the answer."
- *Unlearn the notion that information stands alone, that it is somehow divorced from the person who initiated it or the people who will use it.* The key here is to separate yourself from the idea that you must manage information by itself. Instead, develop a belief that you must facilitate the evolution of that information into knowledge and wisdom, by making it easier to access, to understand, and to retrieve.
- *Unlearn the belief that you must understand every piece of data you're exposed to, that you're somehow less than knowledgeable if you don't.* Remember that empowering involves mutual influence, shared responsibility, and creative distribution of power. You're not alone; you're part of an organization that, as it becomes empowered, multiplies its knowledge by sharing it. What you don't understand, someone else will.
- *Unlearn the feeling that "owning" information gives you personal power.* In reality, the power is in the sharing.

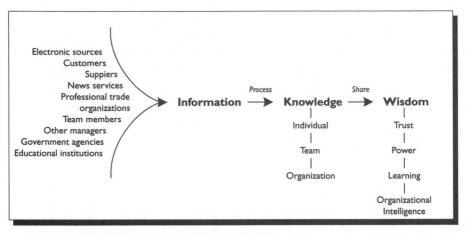

Figure 3-3. From information to wisdom

Hoarding information as a way of controlling others builds barriers to trust, which in turn blocks your growth and that of your organization.

Remember that, no matter what—or rather, who—the source is, information is a resource that you can turn into knowledge and transform into wisdom (Figure 3-3), if you manage it in empowering ways.

## Where Does Knowledge Go?

So you share information, open up the lines of communication in your organization. Information flows! Knowledge increases! Wisdom is on the horizon. Isn't it?

Well, maybe it is and maybe it isn't. Have you ever attended a meeting where someone said, "Remember, we talked about this a couple of months ago, but I've forgotten what we decided"? If you were fortunate, someone in the group actually remembered "what we decided." If you were not fortunate, the group had to relive— repeat—the entire process to arrive at yet another decision.

Michelle ended up on the less-fortunate side in her work with the highway-planning group, as she tells Tom a few months later.

"The Phase 1 road improvements are just about complete, and we just had another meeting to get input from the community before Phase 2 starts," she explains. "But this session didn't go nearly as well as the first one. A couple of new commuters showed up and complained that the sidewalks are an unnecessary waste of the taxpayers' money. They wanted them eliminated from Phase 2—and the new county engineer agreed! Because both the original engineer and the project manager for the construction company have moved on to other jobs, we couldn't find a record of our first meeting or their subsequent consultations—which I'm sure would have provided convincing evidence. I'm appalled at how something that started so well could get off track so quickly."

Just because you widen the avenues by which information reaches you and others in your organization, don't think that you've got the info age "handled." Unless you have fast, reliable ways to record and retrieve information, learning and knowledge may not stand a chance. If you want your organization to grow in wisdom, you've got to include record keeping on your list of empowering actions. Think of it as capturing ideas so that you don't lose them, having information at your fingertips so that you don't have to search for them, recording history so that you don't misplace potentially useful ideas.

Here's a method that worked for one school district. In 10 schools, with 10 very different student populations, teams formed to find solutions to student behavior that is unproductive, disruptive, or just plain dangerous. You can imagine that, at the elementary school level, students' at-risk behaviors are vastly different from those at the high school level, so the teams' membership varies widely, their resources are unequal, their approaches to problem-solving unique. Yet they all follow the same procedure for recording information—and you can too:

1. Use a simple software template and a laptop computer to record meeting notes on the spot and display them on a digital projector or TV screen during the meeting.

2. Summarize data and discussions by topic, by goals, and by actions needed.
3. List action items for each team member.
4. Use the action items from the last meeting as the basis for the next meeting's agenda.
5. Distribute a copy of the notes to all participants, electronically or on paper.
6. Have an "undefined" category in your notes that captures spontaneous feelings or thoughts to be explored later—a parking lot for ideas.
7. Maintain a master archive of meeting notes.

What does such a procedure accomplish? Contrary to what these teams first expected, keeping records actually reduced the length of their meetings—and the volume of their labor—instead of increasing it. Both during and after meetings, they felt clearer about the direction in which they were headed, more informed by more focused discussions, more capable of accomplishing their action items—and more prepared for the next meeting and the next influx of information.

Because of confidentiality constraints, the school teams couldn't go further. But you can. By posting the meeting notes on your intranet, for example, you could effectively archive them in the company database, navigate or search them, and have instant access to past, present, and future plans. But intranet or no, instead

**Smart Managing**

### Make Time for Information

Do you have a time that's dedicated only to sharing information? Many empowering managers do. In one school district, for example, a team meets one morning each week, 30 minutes before the first bell rings. When the bell rings, their time's up.

What do team members think about this arrangement? First, they like the fact that the time is devoted to sharing information: they can ask, suggest, wonder, or consult at this time every week, no matter what. Second, they like the fact that their time is limited: their conversations are more targeted, focused, selective. Third, they like starting the day with new ideas, fresh insights, and food for thought.

of struggling to retrieve information, you'll save time and increase knowledge in the organization by making sure that information goes where it's needed, when it's needed.

Every time the school teams meet, they share existing information and generate new knowledge; they become more educated and they learn; they move from being informed to being wiser. And they don't keep that information, knowledge, and wisdom to themselves. They share it with others, and their individual and collective intelligence grows accordingly. They use the technology that works for them, but not the technology that won't. Is your team doing the same?

## From Techno-Babble to Info-Savvy

Think of valuable information as a renewable resource. The more valuable information you have, the more you can generate. Then the question becomes, as you receive and generate more and more information, how can you heighten its value? How can you practice the *kaizen* approach of continuous improvement with your information?

One way to do so is to ensure that information is as clear and unambiguous as possible. If you move in that direction, you not only move up the empowering manager continuum but also give others a chance to process information more accurately, to convert it into knowledge, and to increase their wisdom and that of the organization.

So, let's talk words. If you worked with us on this book, you'd call yourself an author, wouldn't you? Well, you write reports, letters, emails, proposals, evaluations, or speeches, don't you? You may not have called yourself an "author" before, but you can start now.

As such, we want to share some authoring tips with you (and to reinforce that power-of-information concept).

- *Consider who you're writing for, both those you know about and those you may not know about.* You may think you're writing for experts, for example, people who share a vocabulary and a knowledge base. But what if your "expert" document later becomes the source of a training session for new employees, the basis for a public relations briefing, or the subject of a newspaper article? Think of the time you'll spend "translating" for your new readers. Better to write simply and clearly the first time—and think how much time you'll save when *one* document works for *many* readers.

- *Consider your entire world and the ways in which your organization's intelligence reaches your customers, associates, and suppliers.* Can someone on the opposite side of the globe be expected to understand "insider" jokes, this week's slang, or last year's buzzwords—not to mention your favorite sports analogies? Can you afford to lose a customer, an associate, or a supplier because your language is indecipherable? For example, will "24/7" make sense to everyone who reads your writing? Does 12/7/99 mean December 7, 1999 or July 12, 1999? If you're not sure, you may be inviting misunderstanding.

- *Consider the speed of change and the ways in which meanings change and acronyms multiply.* Have you tired of words like "scenario," "real time," "paradigm," or _____? If you're weary of them, you can logically assume that at least some of your readers are as well. So avoid buzzwords that may not be buzzwords next year (your document may live longer than that). If you must use acronyms, define them at their first occurrence. Don't make your reader guess or run for a dictionary.

- *Consider the "look" of information and how it affects your message.* Ever get a lengthy email that looks like one big box of words, a box you're not particularly motivated to read? Do you want recipients of your messages to feel the same way? Break information into related "chunks" and give each chunk a heading (in all caps, on a separate line, preceded by an empty line, for example). If there's a deadline for response, put it in the subject line—where your reader can see it at a glance—instead of burying it in the body of the email.

- *Consider whether a graphic can replace or enhance your words.* People like pictures. They especially like pictures that have a human element. So if you can insert a simple graphic, perhaps a flowchart or a graph illustrating numerical data, you can save words and will probably enhance understanding.

Remember that empowering is about sharing, creating, and trusting, not about impressing others with your vocabulary. Neither is it about "dumbing down" what you write. Empowering is about communicating clearly on any subject, no matter how complex or how simple. You want others to read and gain knowledge from the information you offer. If you force them to wade through paragraph-length sentences, to translate your underlying meaning from the overlying jargon, to know all the latest acronyms, both of you suffer. You've wasted your time and they feel you've wasted theirs. And you can hardly call what you've done "sharing." Worse yet, the information you wanted to share is lost "out there."

---

### Plain Language

Arthur Levitt, chairman of the U.S. Securities and Exchange Commission (SEC), explains the benefits of the SEC's shift to plain language:

1. Investors are more likely to understand what they're buying.
2. Brokers are more likely to make better recommendations to clients.
3. Companies successfully communicate and develop stronger relationships with investors.
4. Companies save the costs of explaining legalese and dealing with confused or angry investors.
5. Lawyers more easily catch and correct mistakes.

The SEC promotes empowering communication by publishing *A Plain English Handbook* and encouraging public companies to "speak to investors in words they can understand."

## A SPA of Information

**Smart Managing**     Our best advice is this: Keep it Short, Plain, and Active—or SPA—when it comes to information.

Just thinking that *everyone* understands a certain acronym doesn't make it so. What about a new employee, for example, who doesn't know whether POP means "point of purchase" or "post office protocol," whether CRC means "camera-ready copy" or "cyclical redundancy check"?

Just because your Spanish customer speaks English doesn't mean she'll understand your jargon: what does it mean, for example, when your sales go "over the top" or "through the roof"?

Just having something to say that is important doesn't guarantee you an audience. Respect others' time by using fewer, more active words. For example, change "Adjust the environmental control panel by turning the manual temperature tuning cylinder to the off position" to "Move the temperature dial to 'Off.'"

Your words can confuse, muddle, or distort—or they can help transform information into knowledge, knowledge into wisdom, individual data into organizational intelligence.

## Use It or Lose It

Understanding why information is important, how it flows through your organization, and how to clarify it means you have processed data—so you've become knowledgeable about these aspects of information. But knowledge and wisdom come from applying knowledge. Let's revisit Tom and Michelle to learn more. "I'm trying to figure out what I've learned from these highway-design meetings so I can apply it to the way we handle information in our organization," Michelle tells Tom. "I know that I need to work on my information-sharing skills, but I'm not sure how to go about it."

"When you say 'go about it,' I think 'act on it,'" Tom replies. "Why don't we try developing an action plan that will move us in the direction of using information and knowledge for empowering? What if we start by listing the information we have and the information we need to develop a budget for our next project?

It's due next month, and we could accomplish two things at once this way."

"How can I say no, when you put it that way?" Michelle laughs. "Especially since my desk is covered with budget reporting requirements from the comptroller, projections from the project scientist, and demands from the equipment manager. I don't know how to decipher it all."

"Wouldn't our team members need to know about the budget—and couldn't they help us sort what's important and what's not?" Tom asked.

"Of course they could," Michelle said, "and that way, we'd all be 'on the same page' at the same time. Taking this approach also reminds me of something I learned long ago: whenever possible, handle each piece of paper that crosses your desk only once. I'll bring that stack of papers to the meeting, and we'll divide and conquer."

Michelle and Tom indeed took one more step on the road to the empowering organization. They asked their team to share in the information they had. They and the other team members sorted and ranked information from all the budget sources based on its value to the task at hand. They processed the results together—so they benefited from understanding not only *what* each thinks but *how* each thinks. They recorded their conclusions and their plans in simple but complete terms, and they posted their notes on the company intranet so others could use them.

In short, they moved from simply informing to educating and learning, from basic managerial skill to empowering skill—and they added to the organization's intelligence.

## Planning to Inform

As we've said before: empowering *is* certain things and it *does* certain things. And this is the time to do. We recommend that you revisit the "with/without information" list from Figure 3-1, that you look back at your "too much/too little information" list in Figure 3-2, and that you follow Tom and Michelle's lead.

### Develop a Learning Strategy

**Smart Managing**    If you want to encourage and maintain an atmosphere that transforms information into wisdom, develop a learning strategy:

- Share all you know about empowerment, including managing and processing information.
- Create structured and unstructured learning opportunities throughout your organization.
- Keep track of what works, and of how your workforce learns.
- Promote *kaizen:* continuously expand and improve educational activities and opportunities.
- What you'll build with this strategy is a community that learns, one that is resilient, responsive, and competent.

Develop a plan that encourages you to *do* more and better informing, educating, and learning.

Later, ask yourself questions like these to test whether your plan is working.

1. What do you do with a printout from a company database, for example?
   a. Glance at it and toss it aside.
   b. Read it and file it.
   c. Study it and act on the information it contains.
2. How do you use the minutes from a team meeting?
   a. Assign an employee to read them and make a list of the actions I need to take.
   b. Use them to document my attendance for my personnel records.
   c. Evaluate them to remind me what and how my team members think.
3. How do you get information?
   a. Through the company e-mail system, the organization's intranet, the department's online newsletter, the grapevine.
   b. From reading a combination of meeting minutes, transcriptions of conference calls, and professional journals to which my company subscribes.

    c. Through once-a-day, filtered, and sorted email; from just-in-time meetings with supervisors, employees, suppliers, and clients; through select publications or newsgroups.

4. How do you give information?
    a. Verbally, in regularly scheduled meetings with my team or department, whether we need them or not.
    b. In writing, in memo form that is put into each employee's mailbox and sent by email.
    c. In person, with major discussion points or agreements followed up briefly in writing, one-on-one, with my team or across organizational lines.

## The Big-Picture Payoff

In the final analysis, when you act in empowering ways, you share information and increase its value. Someone informs you, your team educates another team, your company

---

### Making Excuses

If you find yourself unwilling to share information, stop and ask yourself why. There are some perfectly legitimate reasons for not sharing: confidentiality, security clearances, and trade secrets, for example. Too often, however, we find some not-so-legitimate reasons to justify our fear that sharing information means losing power.

At a recent professional society meeting, the research committee encouraged members to submit proposals for funding. One participant asked whether samples of successful proposals were available to members, given that such examples could save preparation time and reduce the number of revisions needed for a proposal that wasn't perfect the first time.

"Oh, no," a committee member replied adamantly. "If we show you examples, you might copy them too closely and we'd get proposals that all looked alike."

Was her concern legitimate? Or simply a way to maintain control and the status quo, in which the research committee members hold tight to the information that is the secret to a successful proposal— and the applicants must hope that they can guess the secret? The answer helps us understand whether this is an empowering or a traditional organization.

**Key Term**

**Organizational intelligence** This is information and know-how that is shared throughout the organization. It provides a base for learning more and more and for building organizational competencies and abilities to successfully serve customers. In an empowering organization, intelligence expands as employees and managers learn from one another and build knowledge bases that everyone can access and add to.

learns from its teams. Your organization's intelligence grows and your company increases its viability, its adaptability, its readiness. You reduce the need to relearn, you encourage innovation, and you ensure that your group's history becomes an accessible asset.

There are some aspects of the informing–educating–learning triad that we haven't touched on in this chapter: communication across departmental or organizational "lines," for example, or getting to knowledge and wisdom through training and professional development. We'll be covering those issues in Chapters 4 and 5.

## Manager's Checklist for Chapter 3

❏ Share information regularly with members of your team, department, or organization and create an environment where they share with you.

❏ Regularly sift and sort information effectively and share that which will help people perform better.

❏ Don't handle the same piece of information more than once.

❏ Create systems for recording, storing, and retrieving information that's generated by your team, department, or organization.

❏ Make sure the information and knowledge you contribute is understandable and unambiguous.

❏ Use electronic power and person power to your best advantage to effectively manage knowledge.

❑ Conscientiously contribute to your organization's intelligence and create an environment where others do as well.

❑ Acknowledge the ways that others contribute to organizational intelligence to reinforce their participation.

# Empowering Leadership: Knowing When and How

*We do not need to proselytize either by our speech or by our writing. We can only do so really with our lives. Let our lives be open books for all to study.*

—Mahatma Gandhi

Was managing ever really so simple that one all-knowing, all-powerful executive led a consistently successful, profitable, stakeholder-satisfying organization? Some would say it was, but others would say it never could have been. It is true, however, that some singularly brilliant or charismatic or diligent leader may sometimes set the pace for the rest of us for a while. Ultimately, though, we must rely on our own internal resources and the resources of all the others we work with, whether we're natural-born leaders or blend-into-the-woodwork followers.

Where do you fit into the leadership of an organization that must be highly adaptable, strongly competitive, and increasingly empowering? That's just the building block we want to talk about with you in this chapter. We'll look not only at the quality of leadership but also at the power that comes from expanding leader-

ship across a flatter organizational chart, at how to
decide when to lead and
when to follow and how to
lead in constructive, not
destructive, ways.

> **Empowering leadership**  *Key Term*
>
> Defining empowering leader-
> ship resembles hitting a mov-
> ing target. In empowering organiza-
> tions, leadership will move from one
> individual to another, depending on
> needs, talents, and circumstances.
> Leadership is shared by the formal
> leader, a designated decision maker, and
> informal leaders, who lead on the basis
> of role, task, personal, relationship,
> and/or knowledge power. Both leader-
> ship "faces" may be embodied at times
> in one person and at other times in
> two or more individuals who support
> each other.

We'll also examine how
you can move from a basic
management competen-
cy—decision making—to
first- or second-generation
empowering skills—leading
and transforming. It's an
evolutionary—and you
might say, revolutionary—
process, one in which lead-
ers forgo the isolation of lone responsibility for decisions and
embrace the shared leadership that also expands responsibility.
It's a process in which an expanded base of leaders transforms
the organization and its culture through shared rewards.

## Who's in Charge?

Tom and Michelle are preparing for their next project together.
They've outlined the tasks involved. Now they're choosing the
team members who will work with them. Let's listen in.

"Barry can certainly tackle the integration of work flow and
resource needs, given the way he analyzed the production
department's data last year," Tom is telling Michelle. "Dexter,
over in human resources, understands incentives and the
human resources requirements of this new manufacturing
process, so I think we ought to see if we can include him. And I
think we could use Denise's help in bringing Tonya and Dexter
up to speed on the applicability of the software we installed a
few months ago."

"And who's Tonya?" Michelle asks.

"She was a student intern a couple of semesters ago. She's
just finished her bachelor's degree in business management,

and she's been assigned to shadow me for a few weeks until she refamiliarizes herself with our operations," Tom explains.

"Sounds like we've picked our team, then," Michelle says. "Now I guess we need to find out if they'll pick us—if everyone will be able to give us the time we need from them."

What Michelle and Tom have set out to do is to create an *ad hoc* team, a working group that comes together based on a particular need, not based on department composition or previous group affiliation.

In empowering organizations, leadership doesn't get vested in one particular person—and with good reason. In order to meet the demands of today's fast pace, the faces of leadership often change because the faces of working groups often change. Groups or teams form because they are needed for a particular task. Other groups or teams form because they are wanted, if only by their members, to fill a need among members, such as the need for education or skills training or problem-solving. Still other groups or teams form because they anticipate a future need, and they want to be ready for it. Whether a team forms by directive, by design, or on an ad hoc basis, its leadership is less likely than ever to start and end with one individual. Its leadership is more likely than ever to wear different faces to match a particular task's or project's or organization's needs for a specific or a flexible period of time.

> **Key Term**
>
> **Ad hoc**  Established for a particular purpose. *Ad hoc* indicates being set up to deal with a specific situation and suggests that an action or group is temporary and flexible. The term is often used to refer to teams that form for a special purpose, across department or functional "lines," or as part of an innovative project. An *adhocracy* is an organization that uses ad hoc teamwork to add value to its products and services.

## Formality or Informality?

What's the empowering manager's role in this setting? There are lots of roles you can—and should—play.

For example, in one local chapter of an international profes-sional society, the membership spans five cities and 250 miles. Each year, the chapter holds one meeting in each of the five cities. While the chapter president is the "formal" leader for all five meetings, each city has an "informal" leader who's respon-sible for presenting the program, arranging the site, and com-municating with members about the schedule. If the chapter president can't attend a meeting, the "informal" leader assumes the "formal" leadership role for that period of time.

But whether your leadership role is formal or informal, as an empowering leader, you'll take on lots of roles: trainer of other leaders, adviser to new leaders, consultant to teams, tempera-ture-taker of leadership changes, role model for potential lead-ers, and scout for new leadership talent, just to name a few.

There are other roles as well. Empowering leaders create opportunities for learning. In fact, they think of the workplace as

---

### Taking on and Accepting Informal Leadership

Change is hard. Although some members of a group or team may relish the idea of taking a leadership position when it fits, other members may feel uncomfortable either taking on leadership or accept-ing the informal leadership of others. What should you do? Here are some ideas. Tailor them to the situation:

- Speak in nonthreatening ways. Don't allow a conversation to become a contest or allow yourself to be drawn into an argument.
- Address each individual directly, by name. There's comfort in hearing your own name, and you may smooth some ruffled feelings.
- If you can't resolve the issue comfortably in the group, arrange a one-on-one conversation. Prepare by being rested, open, and ready to lis-ten. Visualize yourself and the other person resolving the issue in spe-cific ways.
- Repeat the other person's objections, using their own words. Be care-ful not to do this in a sarcastic or disrespectful tone of voice, but in a calm and nonjudgmental tone. Sometimes hearing the issue repeated will clarify it for both you and its initiator.
- Ask open-ended questions. Lighten up. Redirect the conversation toward solutions instead of problems.

a learning laboratory where information and people interact to create knowledge and wisdom. Empowering leaders model empowering behavior. They flex, they risk, they experiment, they listen, they reflect, they recognize their own and others' strengths, and they create ways to overcome or work around weaknesses.

## The World Is Flat

Just as leaders come in many different forms, so do organizations. Most organizations are hierarchical, the traditional industrial age model. But we're in the information age now, and this has caused hierarchies to flatten, and employees to take on more authority and responsibility for what they do everyday.

How do things take place in the traditional hierarchy as opposed to the flattened organization? What are the advantages and disadvantages of each? Let's see if Tom and Michelle can shed some light.

"Tonya wants to know who she reports to and who sets her performance requirements," Michelle says to Tom. "She's a little nervous about her place in the organization, and she wants to know who's boss, to put it in her words."

Tom thinks for a moment and replies, "I guess I'd forgotten that things have changed a little around here since Tonya did her internship. Remember, that's when you were still our one-and-only leader, you made all the decisions, and we always brought all our questions to you. No wonder Tonya's confused, now that she's going to be part of an organization where leadership is shared and where everyone takes part in making decisions. Maybe we should think about how to explain the change to her."

> **Key Term**
>
> **Flattened hierarchy** A structural change in which levels of management have been removed because they no longer add value to the organization. Because all employees have ready access to information and can readily communicate with one another, fewer managers are needed to get things done.

What happened next was that Michelle and Tom started drawing, trying to arrive at a picture that would communicate the "traveling" their organization was doing as it moved toward empowerment. Figure 4-1 may give you some ideas as well.

### Leading in a Hierarchy

In a hierarchy, the lines of communication are often few, fixed, and rigid—one-way streets, if you will. For people who don't like ambiguity or uncertainty, that structure suits them better. But it's a structure that slows down decision making and does not allow organizations to respond quickly to customer needs or new market opportunities.

If you're at the top of a hierarchy, you can send decisions and information "down" the organizational chain of command,

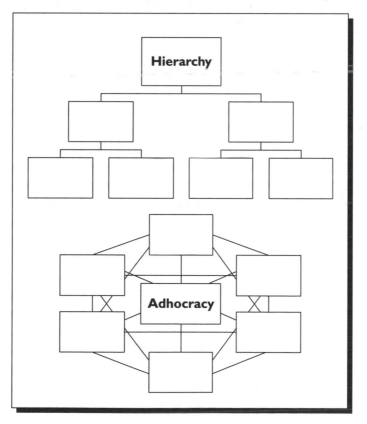

Figure 4-1. Hierarchy or adhocracy?

and if you don't want feedback, you don't have to have it. If you're in the middle of a hierarchy, you're a conduit for decisions and information, passing them from above to below and not necessarily participating in either the decision making or the information sharing. If you're at the bottom of a hierarchy, you don't always understand the reasons for the decisions or the basis for the information that trickles down to you; you do understand that you are expected to meet the expectations of the higher-ups. Often, it's not the organizational norm to question decisions or ask for more information. You just do the best you can with what you've got. The problem is that this limits the ways people can contribute to the organization and limits its ability to take full advantage of what employees have to offer.

In a hierarchy, if you make the decisions, you get the glory when things work out well. When things go wrong, you either accept the blame or pass it down the organizational chart. If you're a middle manager, you may get some credit for the results of good decisions if higher management is benevolent; you may also get the blame for something you had no hand in deciding. If you're at the bottom of the hierarchy, you may never even know what the results were, unless your supervisor decides to let you in on them. It's lonely in this organization, whether you're at the top, in the middle, or at the bottom—but you know exactly where you belong, you know the "rules" for communication, and you can avoid responsibility: if you're at the top, you send it away; if you're at the bottom, you say, "I didn't know." For some of us, one or another of these positions is a perfectly safe and comfortable place to be.

## Leading in an Adhocracy

Perhaps you're thinking that we've exaggerated this hierarchy scenario, and there's some truth there. But bear with us. We've done this to make a point, and we'll balance it with the extreme of the adhocracy scenario. Then we'll temper both points of view with a look at the middle ground, which is where you may find yourself and your organization as you travel the road to empowerment.

An adhocracy makes some people uncomfortable, particularly when they have just arrived from a more traditional hierarchical organization. They don't necessarily have anyone to "answer to," and they often have to find answers for themselves. It may seem there are few rules, and the organizational structure may seem loose or even nonexistent, at least from a traditional point of view. If you were accustomed to being closer to the top in a hierarchical organization, you may feel as though you've lost something—like power or control or visibility. If you were closer to the bottom in a hierarchical organization, you may feel as though you've gained something you didn't ask for and probably aren't prepared for: more responsibility and more accountability.

In an adhocracy, the lines of communication may reach everyone in the organization and move in all directions. In fact, the lines of communication may seem overwhelming, just in terms of the sheer number of people with whom you must communicate. Because leadership shifts on the basis of need or talent, you may be unable to avoid taking a leadership role on occasion, whether you want to or not.

It's difficult to lead in an adhocracy because it's so fluid. However, as you build an empowering organization, it will

---

**Credit and Blame**

Smart managers understand that when things go well in an organization and when things go poorly, it's not usually because of what one person did or didn't do. To understand why and how positive or negative results happen, you have to look at all the steps in the process that yielded those results. Working with employees, evaluate where things are working well and where there are inefficiencies. Learn from that and make improvements, and then continue learning.

**Smart Managing**

---

**Adhocracy** An organizational structure in which there is no strictly defined top and therefore the middle and bottom are also harder to pinpoint. It is a structure where people come together around projects or opportunities and then disperse when their tasks have been completed.

**Key Term**

become more like an adhocracy than a traditional hierarchy. What this means is that as you and your organization move toward empowerment, everyone will have some adjusting to do, whether they have been closer to the top or nearer to the bottom in a hierarchy. As a manager, you'll need to

1. recognize the fact that you and others will need time to make adjustments,
2. promote learning that facilitates the process,
3. help others develop their leadership skills,

## The Secret of the Bottom Line

The team is holding its planning session for the coming year. They're in the second year of a four-year project, so they've done this once before. This time, however, there's a new item on the agenda. Members look to the leader of their group curiously when the time comes to deal with money.

She understands their curiosity and senses some apprehension too. They're thinking, "If the 'secret of the bottom line' is revealed to us, won't we somehow be responsible for it? Is this information we really want to have? Are we ready for it?"

She explains. "We're talking about money today for several reasons. We've spent a year together, learning from each other, taking on differing roles from time to time, turning out a product we're proud of, growing to trust each other's actions and judgment. We've gradually learned that 'secrets' don't give any of us power or control; instead they weaken all of us. Well, money has traditionally been a closely held secret, but it won't be after today."

Team members who had no idea what their benefits added to the project budget learned just what costs their positions incurred. They reviewed the project budget line by line, comparing actual expenditures from the preceding year with projections for the coming year, and revising as their new understanding increased their capabilities.

The bottom line? In the second year, the group saved money over the first, primarily because of the informed suggestions its members made about everything from supplies to contract services. What did they do with the savings? After considering several options—including salary increases—they invested in training that further increased their skills. Their new knowledge enhanced their decision making competency and took them one step closer to empowering leadership skill.

4. tailor your expectations and theirs to a flattened-organization approach, and
5. counsel and support those who are experiencing a change in their leadership role—and get counsel and support for yourself.

Let's get back to Michelle and Tom, who've finished drawing a picture of their new organizational structure for Tonya.

Tom tells Michelle, "I think I'll invite Tonya to talk about her expectations for her new job, maybe give her a rundown on what used to be and what we're striving for now in the way of participation and teamwork. It might help her to better understand how the company is flattening its structure and to get some perspective on how we've changed since she was last here."

"Good idea," Michelle responds. "Let me know how it goes and whether I can be of help. And could you keep your notes so we can use them with other new employees later?"

## To Lead or Not to Lead

Tom's taken the lead by deciding to pursue Tonya's concerns. Deciding when to lead and when not to will be one of the many challenges you face as an empowering manager. Remember, we described *decision making* as a basic managerial competency and *leading* as a first-generation empowering skill. Let's explore the difference between these two skills a little more.

Decision making involves collecting information about a particular situation or issue, generating potential courses of action or choices of behavior, looking at different outcomes, and selecting the alternative that offers the best results. Decision making can be done alone or with others.

Leading can certainly require decision making, but empowering leaders rarely do it alone; they share decision making with others. Empowering leaders also focus on the job at hand, attracting or providing resources, offering experience or insights, asking the right questions, envisioning the ends and the ways in which the means affect people, communicating with everyone who is involved in making the decision or who might be affected by it. In short, an empowering leader, no matter his or her position in the organizational chart, models the organization's beliefs and values (and his or her own), has vision and passion, and takes responsibility for his or her individual performance while sharing responsibility for the group's performance.

### It's Never Too Early

**Smart Managing**    As part of America's Promise, the national program headed by retired General Colin Powell and dedicated to fulfilling promises that give youth the resources they need for successful adulthood, leadership training can start early. For example, high school students learn about team-building skills, interpersonal relations, and conflict management from leaders in business, education, and the military. You and your employees can participate in programs like this one, as a chance to practice what you preach about empowerment, share what you know, and model leadership skills for others who are just beginning to develop them.

As you and your employees become more empowered, you'll probably find yourself leading relatively less often and your employees leading relatively more often. How will you know when it's time to follow? More to the point, after playing the leadership role for so long, will you know how to follow?

## Following the Leader

You can learn to follow just as you learned to lead. Here are a few suggestions:

- Polish your listening skills. Doing so has the added advantage of letting others polish their speaking skills, skills they'll need as they take on leadership roles.
- When others depend on you, offer your support. Don't do the leadership job for them; just make it easier for them to do it. At first, you may need to offer lots of support. Later, you may need to offer less. Still later, you may even find yourself asking for support. (Reciprocation is a great leadership skill.)
- Pay attention to who can teach you something you don't know or something you could learn to do better. Assuming a learning role is a way to shift the leadership role to someone else, without too much effort on your part. Plus—you'll learn something in the process.

### Taking an Interest

Being a good listener requires active participation on the part of the listener. It also requires *taking an interest.*

"To listen well, you must hold back what you have to say and control the urge to interrupt or argue .... Listening is a strenuous but silent activity," according to Michael P. Nichols, author of *The Lost Art of Listening.* Good listening requires suspending your own needs—to control, to advise, to reform—and becoming more empathic (not to be confused with being sympathetic). Empowering managers model leadership by developing their listening skills.

Notice how each of these three suggestions for moving from leading to following is reciprocal. When you move in one direction, that allows someone else to move in the opposite direction. As Joel Barker says in *Paradigms: The Business of Discovering the Future*, "A leader is a person you will follow to a place you wouldn't go by yourself." That definition implies that opportunities await you when you trade leading for following. You'll go places you'd never have gone by yourself.

Don't misunderstand. We're not advocating that you abdicate your leadership position, just that you begin to expand and share it. It will take time. It will take patience. It will take persistence. It will take risk.

But it will mean that you're not alone. It will mean that you have the satisfaction of developing new talent. It will mean that you'll learn from the effects of mutual influence. It will mean that you're relieved of the burden of being a "hero." It will mean that you share responsibility instead of shouldering it.

## Ethics: An Important Leadership Trait

There's one responsibility that increases with empowering leadership: *ethics.* By their position and authority, leaders serve as examples. Since they are in positions of responsibility and authority, they become role models for those they work with and manage. When given the chance to lead themselves, these people will use the behavior of their managers as cues for how they should act and lead. In other words, they look to those behaviors as the standard, as the accepted way to perform, as the way to succeed. People outside an organization—like customers or suppliers—expect that leaders model the organization's values and beliefs, and they judge the organization on that basis.

That's quite a responsibility for managers as leaders in their organizations.  And the consequences of that responsibility become even more significant in an empowering organization. That's when the golden rule of leadership really hits hard: lead as you want others to lead.

So consider how you'll meet the responsibility of serving as a model of ethical standards. Will you say one thing and then act in ways that are contrary to what you say? Will you expect to be excused if you tell a little white lie to gain competitive advantage? Will you excuse others if they do the same? Will you expect it to be accepted if you cheat a little on your travel report because "everyone else does it"? Will you allow an inferior product to leave your assembly line because "no one will ever notice"? Do you want your employees to do the same?

We're not saying you should be holier-than-thou. After all, we all have our human weaknesses. We've all succumbed to temptation, we've all been "too tired to fight it," we've all thought of taking the path of least resistance instead of doing things correctly. But we're trying to move you to be what we think a leader should try to be: a standard-bearer, someone who is an example of one set of whole-life principles. We want you to model leadership that others will want to emulate.

Empowering leaders understand that they have both external and internal customers and that they must present a consistent face to both. Internal customers—employees and peers—will perform in a more committed manner when you have gained their trust and respect. External customers—the people who buy your product or service—will assume you represent your organization and its values and this will affect their decision to do business with you and whether you retain that business.

Sure, nobody's perfect. But don't use that fact as an excuse for not trying to be better. Remember that the concept of continuous improvement applies to leadership qualities too.

## Help Build an Empowering Organization

Every manager finds empowering decision making and leadership a different experience. Regardless of the nature of your organization, you can effect some transformation of organizational beliefs and values through empowering leadership. These tips will help you construct an environment where responsibility and leadership can be shared.

**You're the Role Model** Whether you like it or not, your behavior is what others will use to determine how they should behave. For example, when you listen to others, you communicate that listening is good and inspire others to listen as well. If you look for scapegoats when something goes wrong, others will also do this. So always ask yourself: what model am I projecting? That's the one your employees will use to guide their behavior as well. Make sure you have an intelligent and positive answer to that question.

- *Don't "announce" shared leadership and expect it to happen overnight.* The fact that you've thought about empowerment for a long time doesn't mean that everyone else has. You must provide information, training, and conversation about this new direction. If you already have a process that's participatory in theory, make it participatory in practice.
- *Lose any preconceptions of how a group or team meeting should turn out.* It's easy when you've been in a leadership role for a while to lapse into the habit of presenting questions in such a way as to get the answers you want to hear.
- *If you're a manager who's new to the scene, take time to explore—and respect—the group's existing culture.* Ask questions, acknowledge the value of the group's past, probe for their vision and dreams of the future. Uncovering what's important about the group's business life will keep you out of the potholes on the road to empowerment.
- *Realize that you may have to apply that basic manage-*

> **⚠ CAUTION!**
>
> ### Walk the Talk
>
> Perhaps the single biggest problem of those who would be leaders is not walking the talk. If you model a double standard, others will follow. If you take undeserved credit, if you hoard information, if you make your values conditional on profit or loss, your employees will think this is the way to get ahead and that this is how managers should operate. Further, this is how they will interact with you, hoarding what information they have, blaming you when things go wrong, and they will resent following you. On the other hand, when your words and actions coincide, when you avoid following a double standard, you likewise inspire others to do the same.

*ment competency, decision making, to move your group or team along an empowering path.* Not everyone will want to go. Change isn't always—or often—welcomed, particularly when it's done *to* someone. You'll need to be firmly grounded in your reasons for wanting to move toward empowerment, so you can share that information with others, increase their knowledge, and help them come to understand the benefits that will accrue for everyone by being part of an empowering organization.

- *Expect to fix a flat tire now and then.* As the leading-following roles change hands, as employees practice new leadership skills, as the group or team test-drives its responsibilities, the occasional mishap is bound to occur. Just accepting problems as a natural consequence of empowering—and helping others accept them—keeps the process in perspective.

When Tom talked with Tonya about her expectations for her new job and told her about the recent changes in the organization, he accomplished several constructive things. He's performed as a leader by interacting with her in a positive manner and helping her understand how, by working together, they can better meet some of the organization's goals.

By helping her learn the way in which he operates and by helping her understand why he operates that way, he's modeled leadership for her and given her cues that will help her become a leader as well. He's been responsive to her initial confusion and concern over fitting in and figuring out how the organization functions. She's beginning to understand some of her responsibilities to the team and its participative nature. He isn't forcing her into sharing leadership and responsi-

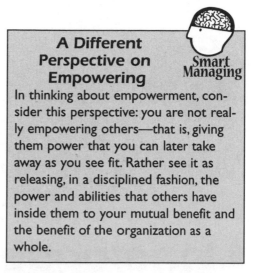

**A Different Perspective on Empowering**

**Smart Managing**

In thinking about empowerment, consider this perspective: you are not really empowering others—that is, giving them power that you can later take away as you see fit. Rather see it as releasing, in a disciplined fashion, the power and abilities that others have inside them to your mutual benefit and the benefit of the organization as a whole.

bility for which she's not yet ready; he is helping her move up the skill path. Both of them come out sharing and winning.

## Manager's Checklist for Chapter 4

❑ Remember that leadership is more likely than ever to wear different faces to match the needs of a particular task or project or the organization for a specific period of time or indefinitely.

❑ Model leadership by creating opportunities for learning, by sharing information, and by following when it's appropriate.

❑ Communicate in ways that demonstrate empowering leadership: move away from few, fixed, rigid lines of communication and toward many, flexible, multidirectional lines of communication.

❑ Take responsibility for your performance and share responsibility for the group's or organization's performance.

❑ Learn to listen. It will help you learn to follow.

# 5

# Who's at Work Here? From Monologue to Dialogue

*Since his days at West Point, Lombardi had based his football philoso-phy on Red Blaik's belief that perfection came with simplicity. The theo-ry was to discard the immaterial and refine those few things that one did best.*

—David Maraniss, *Lombardi's Way*

If hardware gets better and cheaper every month, if software upgrades come too often to keep up, if one day your cus-tomers are in Hong Kong and the next they're in Hoboken, what's constant in your business life? The answer is your human capital. To take full advantage of that capital, become an empowering manager and invest in human capital.

By investing in *human capital*, we mean simply including employees among the capital—the assets—of your team, department, or organization. Normally you might think of assets as just equipment, cash, or real estate, but we're asking you to add the people in your organization to that list. Just as you would upgrade equipment, develop new sources of cash, or remodel your office building, you must ensure that human assets have opportunities to upgrade old skills and develop new ones. You must protect, honor, and value the human investment; in order to do that, you must know who's at work in your organization. To find out who makes up your human capital, you must make a move: from delivering monologues to participating in dialogues. You must become competent in the second building block of empowerment—mentoring and coaching.

How can you make the move from monologue to dialogue, toward investing in human capital? There are lots of ways, but we'll focus on these: knowing yourself, knowing the employees and finding ways to show you care,

> **Human Capital**
> *Human wealth* is what we'd like you to think of when you say "human capital." *First and foremost* is another phrase that conveys the meaning of human capital, because that's where human capital should be on your organization's list of assets: first and foremost. If you mistakenly put other assets at the top of your priority list, you're likely to regret it.
>
> After the 1990s rash of downsizing, reorganizing, and reengineering, smart managers found that human capital is the most valuable of all. Recognize that fact, and it will help you see the intelligence of creating an empowering organization.

developing relationships through language and behavior that's empowering, and learning what it means to coach and mentor.

## Start a Dialogue with Yourself

Dialogue can't truly happen without a relationship, but before you can really get to know someone—develop a relationship with him or her—it's best to know yourself better. So maybe the best place to start a dialogue is with

> **Dialogue** As Dana Zohar so aptly expresses it in *Rewiring the Corporate Brain*, dialogue derives from the Greek *dia* for "through" and *logos* for "relationship," so *dialogue* means "through relationship." As in the dialogues that Socrates had with his students, the ongoing teaching and learning conversation results from questioning and promotes nonconfrontational problem-solving. Dialogue is *not* debate.

yourself. Once you've done that, then you'll be more ready to start one with someone else.

Don't worry, this will be a private conversation. You don't have to talk out loud to yourself, where people might misunderstand what you're doing. Rather, we've provided a way for you to do this in the Management Styles Survey in the Appendix. It will give you some insight into where you stand on the continuum of competencies and skills that empowering managers must cultivate. If you're honest with yourself, the survey will give you a baseline from which you can move toward more empowering behaviors.

Whether you use the survey or not, ask yourself questions about certain aspects of your life, work and otherwise, which we call the six building blocks of empowerment:

- **Informing and learning.** What is it you'd like to know more about so you can be a better manager? Why did you choose these items? Because you think you should? Or because you want to? Make a list and analyze the *should*'s; eliminate them unless you can turn them into *want-to's*. In other words, make learning something you do because you have figured out what you need to know to become a better manager; don't do it because you think you *should* do it to please someone else. (And consider revisiting Chapter 3.)
- **Leading and following.** What does being a leader mean to you? What do you like and dislike about the responsibility of leading? If there are dislikes that you can change, start now; if you can't change them, work on accepting them instead of fighting them. Ask yourself how others feel about your leadership. Is their perception congruent with yours? (If you don't know, start a dialogue with them: ask!) If their perception isn't close to your own, examine the incongruities and act in ways that reduce the difference. (Hint: practice following, and review Chapter 4.) Do you model good followership? Can you ask for the support you need as a follower?

- **Mentoring and coaching.** Knowing your capabilities and preferences in this regard is crucial before you begin a dialogue with someone in your workforce. If you believe that you must do something yourself because "no one else will do it right," don't even think about mentoring and coaching. Instead, have a dialogue with yourself, questioning whether it's fear—and it likely is—that's trapping you. Fear of failure? Fear of losing face? Fear of being seen as less than expert? Fear of giving away power by giving away knowledge? (If it's this last one, go back to Chapter 1. Remember that you actually create power by sharing influence and information.) Name the fear, and you'll be halfway to overcoming it.

- **Providing resources and service.** We're not talking only about doing unto others; we're talking about making sure that you have the resources to take good care of yourself *and* to provide the services that others need. If you're going to respond well to the needs of others, you'll have to do the same for yourself. So, don't deplete your internal resources: give as much attention to your health, both physical and mental,

> ### Coach as Listener
>
> It's the end of the eighth inning. Atlanta Braves pitcher Greg Maddux has been in for the entire game. Coming in from the pitcher's mound, he seats himself next to manager Bobby Cox. The television commentator makes a point: watching the two, there's no question that Maddux is doing all the talking—probably about whether he feels he can stay in for the 9th—and the coach is doing all the listening.
>
> It's a trait all good coaches possess. Cultivate it in yourself. Instead of telling people what they can do, let them tell you. It's the difference between monologue and *dialogue*.

as you do to those who work with you. The stronger your own resources, the stronger source you'll be for others. And the easier it will be for you to ask for help—whether it's supplies, equipment, or people power—when you need it.

- **Structuring and liberating.** As part of knowing yourself, this building block to empowerment asks that you explore what's meaningful about your work. Does your work energize you? Or does it sap your energy? In what ways? What conditions will build the energizing side of the equation and reduce the sapping side? How do you organize, design, or structure relationships and physical space to align with and support each other? Again, answering these questions for yourself will ultimately prepare you to help others find their answers. When our jobs are more meaningful, we're energized—and liberated—to structure them so that we become even more creative, more productive, more value-enhancing. Our personal and professional lives are more fulfilling and our companies' missions are more likely to be realized.

- **Planning and actualizing.** Are you a planner? Or do things just seem to happen to you? If you're going to be an empowering manager, you'll need to know where you stand on this issue—and you'll want to develop your planning skills. Without them, change is something that someone or something else does *to* you. You want to strive to be prepared, be knowledgeable, and be flexible enough to hold your course in the storm of change that inevitably blows your way. In order for planning to become an actualizing experience, you'll need much more than just an up-to-date five-year plan: you'll need a clear vision for yourself and for your organization—and you'll need the time it takes to develop.

Knowing yourself also implies nurturing yourself, your talents, and your skills, before you start trying to help others do so. It's easier to change yourself than to change others. In fact, the only person you really can change is yourself.

## Show 'Em That You Care

Let the changes you make toward empowerment shed light on the process for others. While you're learning to know yourself better, you'll find it easier to know others better—and you'll be able to show that you value them in any number of ways, including these:

- by developing closer relationships,
- by sharing lessons learned,
- by identifying and building leadership qualities in the next generation, and
- by allowing yourself and others to grow beyond current "job descriptions."

What happens when you show that you value yourself and others? You develop mutually supportive—and influential—ways of performing:

- You and others perform better.
- You're there for each other when the going is rough.
- You come closer to building organizational strength and human capital.
- You begin to realize that neither you nor your organization can grow without it.

---

### Evaluating vs. Valuing

**Smart Managing**

What makes you declare someone "worth his (or her) weight in gold"? Well, you might start by saying that gold is a commodity and that weight is something you can count, quantify, or measure. The two, commodity and count, taken together create his or her value. But the empowering manager takes value deeper, including knowing the person and prizing his or her worth on the basis of understanding strengths and weaknesses, talents and needs, insights and blind spots.

It's only when valuing is based on *knowing* that you can truly improve performance. Next time, think of *evaluating* your workers as *valuing* them (*value* is, after all, the root of *evaluate*). Don't rely on counting or quantifying pieces of behavior or goods produced; rely on knowing the individual, knowing the job, and valuing where the two converge. Then you can work on where they diverge.

"Oh, no," you may be thinking, "this is all just too much of a touchy-feely approach to management." But that's not what we mean. You don't have to go out and bare your deepest thoughts and most private feelings to your entire team. But there are two things you do have to do—or rather, things you must not do:

1. Don't play games when you're serious.
2. Don't pretend you're playing games when you're not.

If you're going to start a dialogue, you've got to know yourself. If you're going to start a dialogue, you've got to show them that you care. If you're going to show them that you care, you've got to play straight.

## When You Know, Tell Them

When you're the expert, let it be known. Don't play games with your employees by making them guess—and guess and guess—until they happen onto the "right" answer, which they know you already know. By not sharing what you know, you're cheating yourself, your team, and your organization. They must "play" with you, and it just wastes a lot of time for everyone. You'll never get to the top of the empowering hill if you play coy.

Telling employees what you know is one way to show that you care, one way to start a dialogue (and not too touchy-feely, we might add).

**Smart Managing**

### Spirited Dialogue: Conversations for Change

When you begin a dialogue with others, think of it as having three key characteristics, all of which promote constructive change:

1. Creative: original thought, not just historically accurate judgments.
2. Constructive: shared meaning through efforts to create the future you desire.
3. Appreciative: toward a deeper, richer understanding of each other.

## Strictly Business

A recent letter to *The New York Times* lamented, in effect, "Save me. My boss fell for the advice of a 'team-building expert' and now she asks us to share 'something about yourself that no one else knows' at our staff meetings. I'm terribly uncomfortable with this touchy-feely stuff. What can I do besides alienate my boss?"

Telling everything you know—and asking your workforce to do so—is *not* a way to show that you care. When we speak of "knowing," we don't mean invading someone's personal life. So don't confuse teambuilding and empowering with getting personal with your employees and asking them to get personal with you. It won't work. What you want to focus on is information and ideas that will help everyone perform with more competence and cooperation. In the act of working together in a mutually supportive manner, you and your employees will get to know each other better, and this will reinforce the abilities of people to work together more productively.

## The Sounds of Empowerment

There are at least two other ways to show them that you care: speak in language that's empowering and practice what you speak. In other words, talk the talk and walk the walk.

### The Language of Empowerment

What language is empowering and what isn't? You'll find a starter list below. This list is not all inclusive; it's just designed to stimulate your thinking about how the words you use can undermine or build an empowering environment.

Unempowering language: it stifles awareness and growth. It adds fear of rejection, failure, negativity. Here are some examples:

- *Should have* ... Backward-looking. Condemns a past that can't be changed.
- *Can't, never* ... Gives up before it starts.
- *Worst-case scenario* ... Defeatist. Giving in to fear.
- *I don't want to hear* ... Off-putting. Implies inflexibility.
- *Help me...* Command. May be seen as controlling.
- *I trust you, but* ... Totally mixed message. There's no trust here.
- *My people* ... Implies ownership.

Empowering language: it creates self-awareness and growth. It adds trust, confidence, positivity. Here are some examples:

- *What if* ... Forward-looking. Implies possibilities and creativity.
- *Over, under, around, through* ... Says where there's a will, there's a way.
- *Opportunity-based strategy* ... Futurist. Facing any challenge.
- *I'm listening* ... Engaging. Indicates caring and focus.
- *Would you help me* ...? Query. Usually seen as joint effort.
- *Try it* ... "Trust" isn't here in words. But it's everywhere in the message.
- *We* ... Implies teamwork.

If you have any doubt about your language and its effects, clarify or restate your meaning. There's no guarantee that everyone will understand your intent every time—but at least they'll know you're trying. And they're likely to follow suit.

## Matching Practice to Words

Often, organizations or managers adopt the words of empowerment but they fail to practice what they preach, which means that they fail to empower. Could it be that you have to have certain beliefs and values to talk the talk *and* walk the walk? To make sure your words and actions match,

- Guard against playing office politics.
- Assume everyone can play a role in culture change.
- Keep processes from becoming polarized or battlegrounds for other issues.
- Think of ways to involve everyone.

Here's one more thing to consider about empowering language. Look for ways to make the language in individual's goals mirror the language in the organization's goals. The more individual goals reinforce common goals, the more cohesive the language of the two, the more meaningful they are to both the

individual and the organization—and the greater the
likelihood that they'll be
achieved.

## Go for the Gold

Moving from monologue to
dialogue means moving
from one-way communica-
tion to what we call "two-
way+" communication, a
special kind of two-way
communication and a

> ### Office Politics
>
> There is nothing that can
> undermine an empowering
> environment more than one in which
> office politics—who has power, who
> doesn't; who's in, who's out—comes
> into play. Politics at work breeds cyni-
> cism and discourages employees. It
> encourages game playing, and it under-
> mines commitment. If you want to
> build an empowering organization (or
> even just an empowering work group)
> avoid playing politics.
>
> **Smart Managing**

building block of empowerment: mentoring and coaching. For
many of us, "coaching" conjures up teams, which, in a sports
setting at least, brings competition and collaboration to mind.
Let's pursue this train of thought.

### What Would We Do Without Competition?

Why do we improve our skills, upgrade our wardrobe, tone our
bodies, expand our minds? For many of us, at least part

> ### Matching Goals to Goals
>
> **Smart Managing**
>
> The more closely individual goals align with organizational
> goals, the more likely individual accomplishments will add
> value to organizational products and services. Translation: happier cus-
> tomers, bigger bottom line.
>
> Review the language of your team's or your department's personnel
> evaluation system. Does it encourage language that reinforces organi-
> zational goals? Does it use clear, concise language to express those
> goals, hence performance expectations? Does each employee get to
> "see" how the talk and the walk match?
>
> For example, in one school district, each school has an improve-
> ment plan. Each improvement plan's goals are directly tied—visibly in
> chart form and verbally in the plan's language—to state education
> goals. Each team's goals are tied to the school improvement plan in
> the same way. In each case, the language reinforces the actions, individ-
> ually and organizationally.

of the process of continuous improvement (remember *kaizen?*) is motivated by competition. So although the word "competition" sometimes gets a bad name, you might want to consider its good side.

As Harvey Robbins and Michael Finley point out in their book, *TransCompetition*, competition can make us feel compelled, excited, fulfilled—or make us feel dread, fear, sorrow. These feelings are why some of us swear by competition, while others swear *at* it.

**Competition** A test of skill, ability, or talent, *competition* connotes that someone wins and someone loses. If you're with us in believing that empowering managers get beyond win-lose to win-win, that connotation stops you in your tracks. If, however, you consider that competition raises the bar, motivates us to strive for continuous improvement, and energizes us to innovate—well, it doesn't sound so bad, does it?

We're going to ask you to talk to yourself again. Before you decide whether you're ready to mentor and coach, ask yourself whether you and your protégés are actually *competitors*.

- Do you feel threatened by their expertise, for example?
- Do they feel it necessary to "best" you in order to develop their own careers?
- Do you spout empowerment but act like a benevolent dictator?
- Do they believe that in order for them to win, you must lose?

If you answered yes to any of these questions, read on. Collaboration may help overcome some of the down sides of competition.

## What Can We Do with Collaboration?

Whether we use competition or do away with it, we certainly can do empowering things with collaboration, including creating dialogues. Figure 5-1 shows how.

Before you go further, talk to yourself one more time. Will your mentoring program be open to all employees or only to a

| Competition | Collaboration |
|---|---|
| • Proclaims winning "hero"<br>• Rewards individual effort<br>• Creates value for one<br>• Achieves individual goal<br>• Celebrates independence<br>• Reinforces career "ladder" | • Shares winning and power among all<br>• Rewards mutual influence and accountability<br>• Creates value for organization<br>• Achieves organizational goals<br>• Promotes interdependence<br>• Builds career development |

Figure 5-1. Competition and collaboration

select few? What message does selectivity send? A collaborative one or a competitive one? Does your mentoring program intend to produce "stars" or "heroes" or will you foster a team effort? Will your mentoring activities stem from a genuine desire for dialogue? Or will you be delivering monologues?

If you want answers to these questions, you'll have to talk to yourself. The answers depend on where you are on the empowering continuum. And the answers depend on where you want to go. You may want to revisit these questions after you learn more about coaching and mentoring.

> **Collaboration** "To work, one with another; to cooperate," according to *Random House Webster's College Dictionary*. Collaboration involves problem-solving, process improvement, and change management, as Kyle Dover maintains in an article in the January 1999 *Management Review*, "Avoiding Empowerment Traps." Those two sources work together to provide a solid definition of *collaboration*.

## Olympic Challenges

Think about it: isn't good coaching simply good managing? We think so, as does Patricia Fritts, in her book *The New Managerial Mentor*. She says that mentoring management is an approach that ensures the continuous investment in human capital, that guarantees you'll learn as much as you teach, that promises leadership for your organization's long haul. With mentoring management:

### The Meaning of Mentoring

If we had to define *mentor*, we'd define it in terms of a person and the relationships of learning, trust, and knowing that he or she builds. One person comes to mind immediately.

An 80-year-old attorney, too invigorated by his work to retire, spends the first hour of his morning "roaming the halls." Where he stops each day varies; nevertheless, his purpose is always the same. He spots someone he's not talked to for a while, often a young associate, checks to see whether the timing is OK, then joins that person in his or her office for a chat (dialogue, if you will). If he's questioned, he shares what he knows. If he's the questioner, he listens wholeheartedly to the response. If he hears a need, he offers potential resources for filling it; better yet, he helps the other party arrive at options.

In short, he's available, he's attentive, and he's supportive. He learns from those younger than he, and others benefit from his experience. It doesn't eat up a tremendous amount of anyone's time, but his advice is timeless.

- You'll act as an expert resource.
- You'll be a source of organizational history and experience.
- You'll offer a broader perspective than what your protégé might otherwise experience.
- You'll be a facilitator, someone who understands dialogue and who's a skilled listener, someone who builds relationships that help others perform more effectively together.
- You'll lead the way to develop relationships and learning networks, within your organization and outside it.
- You'll help pinpoint problems, find resources, and spread information.

Without learning leaders like you (who, you'll remember, also know when to follow), no organization can achieve the transformation that comes from empowerment.

As a mentor and coach, you won't be the parent to a "son" or a "daughter." In other words, you won't see your role as being a parent or boss, with all the negative connotations that attach to those terms. Rather, you're a partner in the creation of an empowering organization with the goal of improving everyone's performance, including your own.

Regardless of how much change you face, no matter how often you hear that managers' jobs are quickly disappearing, in spite of the fact that you'll never know everything you

> **Coach** In *Delivering on the Promise: How to Attract, Manage, and Retain Human Capital*, Brian Friedman, James Hatch, and David M. Walker call a *coach* someone who provides "potential styles and tools for increasing performance," someone who facilitates learning, someone who's a skilled listener, questioner, summarizer, action-feedback giver, inspiration, model, brainstormer, joint problem-solver—most often a line manager.

need to know, as a manager, you must realize ways in which *you* add value for your company's customers. And one of the most important ways of doing that is by helping others understand what you know, how you know it, how to make time to think (both deeply and on the run), how to tap into the organization's intelligence—in short by leading, coaching, and mentoring.

You're likely to find yourself mentoring more than one person, and you're likely to find yourself mentoring in some new ways. Here's one example.

Mentoring, like everything else these days, is going digital. People who can communicate electronically, through an intranet or the Internet, can share their expertise and their concerns, their experience and their questions, meeting in spirit if not in space and time.

*E-mentoring* can also connect strangers. Through the World Wide Web, fledgling professionals can establish contact with experienced professionals. There are Web sites that allow visitors, in what some call a "matchmaking service," to search for a mentor with particular skills, one who answers questions or discusses concerns free of charge. Although some suggest that the best mentoring occurs when people are face to face, e-mentoring offers speedy communication between people who aren't in the same location.

Whether you're in the next room or the next country, does e-mentoring accomplish what you'd want to accomplish in a face-to-face mentoring relationship? Here are just a few issues to consider when you're deciding whether e-mentoring delivers on the promise of mentoring:

- Does e-mentoring give you the opportunity for the kind of feedback that's full of information? A smile, a wrinkled brow, a gesture, a pause? If mentoring is about building relationships, can you do it on the Internet? Ask someone who's developed a successful romance on the Internet, and you'll get a resounding "Yes!" Ask others who've been cheated in one way or another—romantically or otherwise—and you'll get a "No." We suggest that perhaps the truth lies somewhere in between.
- Does e-mentoring deliver speedy—and relatively short—responses to both simple and complex questions? Yes, if you're satisfied that mentoring is simply an "answer for every question" proposition. No, if you think mentoring goes beyond the Q&A arrangement.
- Does e-mentoring allow mentor or protégé to avoid each other—or sticky issues—if the relationship hits a snag? There are bound to be times when you'd welcome the chance to avoid someone as easily as you can on the Internet. "Our server went down." "They dumped our message queue last night." "Gosh, I don't know why that message didn't go through." Sound familiar? The question is whether your mentoring relationship profits from avoidance. We think the answer is "No."

Whether you're a firm proponent or opponent of e-mentoring, or whether you're straddling the fence, if you do find yourself using it, be certain that both parties get what they need and what they expect from this e-relationship. Discussing those needs and expectations—remember, this is a mutually influential arrangement—and establishing some ground rules for e-mentoring goes a long way toward empowering the experience. There will be times when a quick answer to a simple question is all that's needed; at other times, nothing else but a lengthy, face-to-face conversation will do. Just be sure you've given yourselves the options you need.

Whew, we've had quite a dialogue. Keep it up, whether you're talking with yourself, coaching a particular skill one-on-one, or e-mentoring an entire department. Use it to evolve from a traditional managerial position to an empowering managerial role. One last word of caution: don't confuse dialogue with debate—or you'll find yourself back at square one, delivering a monologue.

What's empowering about if it's not about striving for high, sustainable performance? In Chapter 6, we'll map resources and services to the needs and aspirations of high performance organizations. We hope you'll travel along.

---

**Dialogue or Debate?**

Consider how dialogue and debate differ, according to Dana Zohar in *Rewiring the Corporate Brain*:

| **Debate** | **Dialogue** |
| --- | --- |
| • is rule-bound | • requires open minds and hearts |
| • is formal | • includes emotions and intellect |
| • says, "I know I'm right" | • suspends certainty |
| • requires you to defend a position | • is about finding out |
| • ends in defeat or victory | • ends in new knowledge or insight |

Be aware of the differences, and you'll do more dialoguing and less debating.

---

## Manager's Checklist for Chapter 5

❑ Invest in human capital, making it first and foremost on your organization's list of assets. Just as you would upgrade equipment, develop new sources of cash, or remodel your office building, you must ensure that human assets have opportunities to upgrade old skills, develop new ones, or remodel existing ones.

❑ Remember that *dialogue* means "through relationship." As Socrates did with his students, realize that ongoing, teaching and learning conversations result from questioning and promote nonconfrontational problem-solving. Dialogue is *not* debate.

❑ Consider competition and collaboration before you begin coaching and mentoring. If you're competing with a potential protégé, resolve those issues first.

6

# What's at Work Here? Process vs. Results

*It is better to know some of the questions than all of the answers.*
—James Thurber

You might have wondered whether we put our money where our mouth is when it comes to the terminology of empowerment. What we're referring to is our continued use of words like *workforce* or *employee* or *manager*, words that seem to perpetuate a distinction between people at different levels of an organization—levels that we keep telling you will be less important in an empowering organization.

While we've cautioned you against terms like *my people* or *subordinates*, we continue to make distinctions because, as we've also said before, empowerment is a process—not an event. So it's likely that there will always be some sort of distinction among individuals who work in organizations, among those who travel different routes toward empowerment, whether that distinction is based on specialized skill sets, the remnants of a hierarchical "position," or membership in a particular ad hoc team. This doesn't mean that people won't still have different levels of responsibility and authority, but these levels are not there to reinforce a hierarchy but facilitate the smooth working of the organization.

All of this goes a long way around saying that we'll be using *workforce* and *employee* and *you* a lot in this chapter. And although those words may make it sound as though we're distinguishing between *you* and *them*, we're not. *You* are included with *them*; when we say *workforce* or *employee* or *them*, we mean *you* as well. Together, we'll explore the value of finding out what makes each of us "tick" at work—and why we should want to know and what to do once we do know.

With that said, let's talk about surveying employees, so you can better match their needs and wants to organizational resources and services to make them more productive and better able to satisfy customers.

## Just Tell Me What You Want

Why should you be interested in what employees know, need, and want? What do you get when you ask employees what they want? These are the questions that will help you build a firm foundation for another important aspect of empowerment: providing services and resources for a workforce that adds more value for you and for your customers.

As a manager, you've probably had at least one experience like the one that Tom and Michelle had in one of their team meetings. Let's listen in.

"We don't know exactly how to sugarcoat the information we're about to share with you," Tom tells the assembled team members, "so we'll just blurt it out. The home office just announced that they're installing an entirely new—and different—voice mail system company-wide. It will mean that we'll have to give up the training session we had scheduled for next week because it would have conflicted with the time the company has scheduled training for us on the new system."

"No way!" Denise reacts. "We've planned for that training session for months. It's something we really need, and given the demands of our latest project, we won't be able to work it in again until next quarter. What do they mean, committing us to something without even asking?"

"Besides," Arlo pipes up, "the voice mail system we have works just fine anyway."

Pretty easy to detect the emotions at this meeting, wouldn't you say? We suspect they mirror what yours would have been in a similar situation. Surprise, anger, disgust, frustration, just to name a few. Not, we also suspect, the kinds of feelings you want to provoke—at least not when they easily could have been avoided.

As you might well imagine, Tom and Michelle are at a loss to explain the behavior of their "superiors." This is the perfect example of behavior that you want to avoid. Although planning is a basic management competency, planning *for* people instead of *with* them is less than competent. What actions would have avoided this situation and the accompanying reaction? Easy: ask people what they want, what they need to do their jobs, what ideas they have about certain choices—and ask them before the decision is made. (Simply asking helps make decision making an experience in mutual influence. Even if the decision is different from what some employees most wanted, when they've had a voice, they're more likely to accept a decision, whatever it is.)

Have we made our point? Michelle and Tom's experience is also the perfect example of why you should want to know what your employees think, want, and need.

---

**Beware Silence**

Henry Tam, director of the Cambridge Centre for Citizenship Development, points out three obstacles to empowering strategy: lack of commitment from the top, too little understanding, and *staff silence* (or lack of feedback).

So beware if your employees keep their opinions, ideas, and feelings to themselves. Whether such silence results from fear, cynicism, or apathy, it can throw up impassable roadblocks to empowerment.

Source: Henry Tam, "Empowerment: Too Big a Task?" *Professional Manager*, March 1994.

### What Do You Get When You Ask?

What do you get when you ask what employees want? You get increased employee satisfaction. It's as simple as that. It's automatic. The mere fact that you've asked what someone thinks or wants or believes—regardless of the outcome or response—is enough to improve your relationship. Why? Asking shows caring, concern, openness to ideas, willingness to change, commitment to dialogue—in short, asking shows trust. And trust given can't help but be reciprocated.

> ⚠️ **CAUTION!**
>
> **Asking and Trusting**
>
> If you expect *asking* to generate *trusting*, you've got to ask in a trusting way. You can't "load" a survey with questions that force the response you want to hear. You can't have behaved in distrusting ways for years and then expect trust to follow immediately on your first "new" approach to surveying employees. You can't use the results of a survey to punish, to cajole, to try to mold someone's attitude or opinion to your own.

So if you're going to be a manager who rises above mere competence, who moves from *directing* employees to *providing* resources to employees, you're going to want to survey those employees. You're going to be rewarded with automatically increased employee satisfaction—if you follow up *asking* with *acting* on the answers you receive.

Now, you might be wondering, what do you ask, how do you ask, and when do you ask?

*What* you ask depends on what you need to know and where you are on the continuum of empowerment. *How* you ask, not surprisingly, also depends on what you need to know.

For example, "What do you see as our organization's mission?" might come very early in your empowering journey, affording you the chance to see whether and how closely the workforce and management are aligned. You'll then know whether you have lots of work to do in establishing a cohesive corporate vision. "What have you learned from our empowerment efforts?" could come early in the empowering process or it could come later. Both are *open-ended questions* that allow for open

## Asking and Trusting, Part II

Before beginning work on the development of training manuals for a national organization of appraisers, the training developers decide to survey organization members. They ask questions about understanding of pertinent regulations, about job satisfaction, about goals and missions—and they promise survey participants anonymity.

After all the results are in and tabulated, the developers meet to review them. One survey question stands out from the others as evoking lots of emotion. The developers review individual responses to the question and one of them says, "I think I'll call this fellow and find out just what he means by his response. It would really help me to know what's behind his thinking."

Fortunately, the other developers—to a person—object. "When we asked people to respond to these questions," one of them explains, "we made a pact with them. We guaranteed them anonymity. No matter how much it would help us to dig deeper, we can't violate that trust."

"What we could do," suggests a third developer, "if this new information is genuinely critical to our putting out a good product, is to send out a second survey. We could explain that the first survey raised other questions and we'd like their answers. That way, we maintain the trust we've begun to build, and we get the information we need."

answers of any length, quality, or style. Employees who respond to questions like these are likely to feel that their opinions are valued, that they are free to contribute more or less, depending on their personal preference, that they are party to a dialogue.

Asking, "Should we reconsider our current customer service approach?" takes the *closed question* tack, forcing employees to answer "yes" or "no," with no room for originality or creativity—or information. If, however, you follow that closed question with a more open-ended (but focused) one—"If 'yes,' why? If 'no,' why not?"—you'll again open lots of doors and you'll get lots of information.

As you proceed toward building an empowering organization, imagine what you could do with the results from this question: "If you don't have all the information you need to do your job, what can your manager do to help you get it?" Not only do you show that you value employees' opinions, you also show your willingness—and your commitment—to working with them toward continuous improvement. And you leave no doubt about your intent to behave as a servant-leader.

And finally, asking, "What haven't we asked that you think we should?" or "What would you like us to know that we haven't thought to ask?" will get you information you never even dreamed you might be missing. Try it! It just might change your next survey for the better.

*When* you ask, as you've seen in the preceding examples, can be any time—whether you've just started work toward empowerment or you've been working toward empowerment for a long time. Maybe the more pertinent question is *how often* do you survey employees?

It's a cinch that once a year is not enough. In a study described in *Organizational Behavior and Human Decision Processes* (April 1999), a Purdue University psychology professor, Howard Weiss, found that daily events have the greatest impact on how we feel about our work: "Too often organizations assume that employees' feelings are constant. Actually, workplaces are more like emotional cauldrons, with daily circumstances influencing employee feelings and job performance."

### Fast—and Usable—Results

A major auto maker uses an automatic e-mail survey/response system. On a daily basis, the e-mail survey pops up on each employee's computer screen. Questions are short and straightforward, but there's room for free-form, written comments as well.

Results are processed instantly, and reports are available immediately. Immediacy is the advantage of this technique and when managers act on what they find, this sends a fast message to employees that managers are listening and acting on employees' ideas and concerns.

## What Do You Get When You Increase Employee Satisfaction?

So you increase employee satisfaction by asking what they think, what they want, and what they need. So what? Does the process stop there? Or does it reach deeper to your customers? The truth is that what you get with increased employee satisfaction is increased customer satisfaction—another "simple as that" cause-and-effect kind of experience. Let's talk about this a little more.

As Ken Blanchard asks in "Servant-Leadership Revisited," an essay in *Insights on Leadership* (ed. Larry C. Spears), "Who do people think they work for?" If they operate in the pyramid of a hierarchy and if they think they work for the person "above" them, their energies are directed—where? Why, up the corporate ladder, of course. The people they have to please are the ones "up there," aren't they?

Now, here's a change in perspective. What happens if, in your mind if not yet in reality, you turn the pyramid of hierarchy upside down? Now, who's on top? Your customer! Who's next in order of importance? The employee whose efforts affect your customer. Who's at the bottom of the hierarchy? Management. "Now, who works for whom?" is the logical next question, in Blanchard's example (Figure 6-1).

Surprised? Actually, we're kind of relieved—because we've finally arrived at the most important point in this chapter of our empowering journey. That's the fact that empowering managers serve the employees by providing the tools, information, support, and training that employees need to do what they're

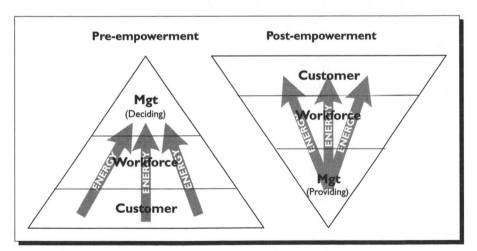

Figure 6-1. The flow of energy, pre- and post-empowerment

supposed to do: fulfill customer's needs and expectations. But they can't do it without managers' help.

## Tooling Up for Servant-Leadership

When you ask employees what they think and what they need, you're going to find out about your employees—*and* you're going to find out about your *customers*, aren't you? Who better to tell you about your customers' needs than the people who face them every day? And while you're tooling up to respond to the needs of your employees so they can respond to the needs of your customers, you might just begin to think of yourself in a new role: that of *servant-leader*.

Do the terms *servant* and *leader* seem at odds? Perhaps at first glance, but not if you buy into the notion that leadership is earned by the leader and bestowed by followers, based on the capacity and intent of the leader to serve, first and foremost.

What does this concept of servant-leader mean to you as an empowering manager? It means simply that you will offer resources when workers need them to do their jobs, when cus-

### The Sound of Top-of-the-Pyramid Employees

How employees act with customers depends whether your pyramid is traditional or inverted, on whether managers serve their employees or expect the employees to be serving the managers.

When you serve your employees by providing them with resources that support those ideas and needs, you'll hear employees talk to customers like this:

"We'll find a way."

"I'll be glad to help you."

"I have all the time you need to find a solution."

When, instead, you act as the person who needs to be served by your employees, you'll hear them talk to customers like this:

"It's out of my hands."

"I can't help you with that."

"I'm sorry, but I can't make that decision."

You choose. Which would you prefer to hear?

**Servant-Leaders** Leaders who understand their role is to facilitate the success of those they lead—in other words to serve them. This term was coined by Robert K. Greenleaf, eminent leader at AT&T and founder of The Center for Applied Ethics (later The Greenleaf Center for Servant-Leadership). As Greenleaf explains in his book, *The Servant as Leader*, "It begins with the natural feeling that one wants to serve, to serve first. Then conscious choice brings one to aspire to lead .... The difference manifests itself in the care taken by the servant—first to make sure that other people's highest priority needs are being served."

As Larry C. Spears puts it in his essay, "Tracing the Growing Impact of Servant-Leadership," in *Insights on Leadership*, "True leadership emerges from those whose primary motivation is a deep desire to help others." It only makes sense. Would you want to follow a leader who did not have concern for you and your success? Think about it.

tomers need them to be satisfied, when innovation requires new supplies. It means you'll find a way to get the job done. It means that you'll ask for input from your employees so often and with such honesty that you'll begin to *anticipate* when, where, and what sources of time, money, materials, and information they need.

You'll be *serving* your employees and your customers alike. You'll be *leading* by making it possible for employees to do more than they ever expected they could. Together, you'll be adding value to products and services—and you'll be ensuring the resilience and longevity of your organization.

## Access and Expectations

Now we've covered what employees can come to expect from you when you behave as a servant-leader. What, you might be wondering, can you expect from employees who see you as a servant-leader? Here are some answers to that question from Ken Melrose, CEO of Toro, from "Putting Servant-Leadership into Practice" (*Insights on Leadership*):

- Employees won't wait for you to tell them what to do, because you'll have turned their requests for your single-handed decisions into shared learning and decision making experiences. (Remember about creating power through mutual influence?)

- Employees will risk more, create more, trust more, because you'll be accepting of their mistakes, supportive of their learning from them, and interested in their points of view. (Remember to survey the employees!)
- Employees will support the organization's values and mission by their actions and words, because you will clarify, share, and discuss the values and mission with them and because together you will establish goals that move each of you closer to achieving that mission. (Remember *kaizen*, the concept of continuous improvement?)
- Employees will feel valued, and their performance will reflect that feeling, because your service—and your leadership—will be the visible, tangible implementation of the belief in leader as servant, the proof that the customer and the employee are at the top of the organizational pyramid, not the bottom. (Remember the change in perspective.)

## The Sustainable Organization and the Servant-Leader

Serving your employees is all well and good, you may be thinking. A happy worker is a productive worker. But we'd like to intrude on your thoughts once more, to remind you that the customer is the ultimate beneficiary of successful servant-leadership.

We've said it before, but it bears repeating. If your organization's journey toward empowerment doesn't result in products and services that better satisfy and even delight customers and help the company grow and prosper, what are you in business for?

If you want to continue to reap the rewards of empowerment, you've got to act in ways that sustain your organization and the people who *are* the organization.

Just what do we mean by sustainability? And how can you attain it? Let's talk more about that.

If you haven't guessed by now, we think you *must* find out what employees think, want, and need if you're going to build a sustainable organization.

Here are some other ways to build a sustainable organization.

### Bottom Line: Think Three

Usually we think of the *bottom line* as being in one place, on a financial statement, and coming in (we hope) one color: black. But empowering managers look beyond one place and one color. Instead, they see three bottom lines: *social*, *human*, and *financial*. The *social* bottom line, according to Jane Galloway Seiling in *The Membership Organization: Achieving Top Performance Through the New Workplace Community*, shows an organization's public responsibility, product integrity, environmentalism, and purposeful philanthropy. The *human* bottom line shows how the organization treats it employees, whether it invests in training, whether it treats the workforce fairly or unfairly. The *financial* bottom line shows ... well, you know that one. And the fact is that they all support one another.

- Reward innovation and creation instead of damage control.
- Promote ownership of the whole organization, not just your "part" of it.
- Have more "fun to do" and less "have to do."
- Aim for smaller but more frequent paoffs versus one big payoff at "the end." (And remember, there's really never an "end" anyway.)
- Concentrate on what you are and what you do (remember "Empowering is ..." and "Empowering does..."?) instead of what you give and what you take.
- Find "the good life" inside the organization instead of seeing it as something that happens only outside the organization.
- Take pride in what you and others accomplish within a reasonable amount of time, instead of commiserating (or worse, bragging) about how much you work over-time.
- Create an organization that's a healthy place for the people who constitute it—for their bodies and for their souls.

## The Three R's of Empowerment

Think back to the reaction of Tom and Michelle's team when they heard that a decision had been "handed down" without any

> **Key Term**
>
> **Sustainable**  A sustainable organization is one that survives and grows through time. It is one where everyone understands the importance of being a good business citizen and of continuously improving internal processes and the quality of goods and services delivered to customers. It is one where there is a long-term mutually beneficial relationship between customers and organization.
>
> If you break *sustainable* into its parts, you have *sustain* and *able*. *Sustain* means support, endure, keep up, supply with necessities, furnish with means or funds, aid, uphold, confirm. Add *able* to this list and you begin to picture an organization of servant-leaders, an organization that endures, that's resilient, that's built to last.

thought to asking for their opinions, feelings, and knowledge. What was missing from the way the organization treated these employees? Why did they feel they'd been treated unfairly instead of fairly (one measure of the *human* bottom line)?

We believe it's because the organization forgot to treat them with *respect* (by asking), neglected to give them *resources* they needed (instead of ones they didn't), and lost track of the fact that *reinvestment* in the employees—the people who make up the organization—is probably the single most effective way to create power and lasting, successful enterprise. Here's another example of what can happen if you forget the three R's of empowerment.

In a survey by the U.S. General Accounting Office conducted in 1998 and 1999, Navy and Air Force pilots responded in some surprising ways. The President and the Joint Chiefs of Staff chairman lobbied Congress for a pay raise they assumed would improve morale and retention, but the pilots would have preferred spare parts for their planes. They simply wanted the resources needed to do their jobs well.

So the next time you consider ways to motivate employees, to increase your customer base, to build sustainability into your organization, *ask* people what they think, what they need, and what they want. The act of asking shows respect, allows you to provide resources, and helps you reinvest in the most valuable bottom line you've got: the human one. It only follows that the energy in your organization will begin to flow upward in your new pyramid: toward serving the customer and the employee, both of whom need you to be successful, too. And that leaves you in an empowered position, too—that of servant-leader. Who knew it could feel so much better to be at the bottom instead of the top?

> **A Passion to Serve**
> Why would you want to be a provider, a resource-finder, a source of energy, time, and supplies for employees? Perhaps the best way to answer that question is to quote Joe Batten, who says it best in his essay, "Servant-Leadership: A Passion to Serve," in *Insights on Leadership*: "Go-getters ultimately get got. Go-givers ultimately become rich in every way."

## Manager's Checklist for Chapter 6

❑ Ask what your employees think, need, and want. What do you get? Increased employee satisfaction, for one thing. The mere fact that you've asked what someone thinks or wants or believes—regardless of the outcome or response—is enough to improve your relationship.

❑ Who better to tell you about your customers' needs than the people who face them every day? Just one more reason to survey your employees!

❑ While you're asking, ask yourself who's on top of your organization's pyramid? If you've adjusted your thinking toward empowerment, it's your customers! Who's next in order of importance? Your employees. Who's at the bottom? Management. Now, ask yourself who works for whom?

❑ Remember that the bottom's a great place to be. You're needed, your capacity to build and support the organization is recognized and appreciated, and your employability is enhanced. You've shown that your skills sustain the organization's foundation.

❑ Remember that leadership is earned by the leader and bestowed by followers, based on the capacity and intent of the leader to serve, first and foremost. Being a servant-leader means that you offer resources when workers need them to do their jobs, when customers need them to be satisfied, and when innovation requires new supplies; that you'll find ways to help get the job done; that you'll ask for input; and that you'll *anticipate* needs.

❑ Don't forget the three R's of empowerment: treat employees with *respect*, give them *resources* they need, and *reinvest* in employees—the people who make your organization a powerful, lasting, successful enterprise.

# No More Reengineering: Make More with What You've Got

*The wave of the future is not the conquest of the world by a single dogmatic creed but the liberation of the diverse energies of free nations and free men.*
—John F. Kennedy

Some things in life we can control; others we can't. We've talked earlier in this book about the fact that the *power* in *empowerment* is not about controlling other people, that it's about creation and sharing and transformation with other people. But along the road to empowerment, you'll come across issues and decisions that you and your employees do have control over—and exercising that control will create power.

One of those powers is structuring your work environment, in terms of both space and relationships. By creating an empowering structure in your office space and your office communication, you actually liberate the energy, enthusiasm, and empathy that make work a good place to be.

This *structuring* building block of empowerment is the one that takes into account the social characteristics of life in your organization. And it's the one that builds and supports that mini-society.

So put on your hard hat. We're about to become structural engineers at the empowerment-building job site—or choreographers on the great stage of life, if you prefer.

## Turn Reengineering into We-engineering

The business world is fraught with terminology that comes and goes—often along with the short-lived programs it describes— and *reengineering* is definitely a term that captured managers during the '90s. Just what does it mean? There are lots of different definitions, but typically reengineering refers to revising business processes to adjust for the rapid change we all experience. Often revising existing business processes includes installing new or upgraded technology.

> **Key Term**
>
> **Reengineering** The fundamental rethinking and often radical redesign of business processes to achieve dramatic improvements in areas such as cost, quality, service, and speed. Often such change occurs because of or requires new technology.

It's been said often enough that we human beings resist change, but does that necessarily make the statement true? Could it really be that what we're resisting is not change itself but the fact that we're not consulted about change that affects us?

Which leads us to our point. We'd like you to reconsider the next time you reengineer. We'd like you to *we*-engineer instead. When you engineer something, you design, construct, or use it. You can't do that without taking into account how what you do will affect employees, and if you don't take that into account, they *will* resist whatever change you throw at them. (That's what you'll be doing, you know: throwing change at them or manipulating them.)

What can you do to make we-engineering part of your organizational structure? You can consciously and conscientiously— not accidentally or haphazardly—design, construct, and use organizational space and relationships in empowering ways.

## Rethinking, Reengineering, Renewal

Kyra, a manager from research and development, is paying a visit to Tom and Michelle. She looks worried.

"We just discovered that three months' worth of our engineers' time-control cards were hidden away in the bottom of someone's desk. I think they were trying to prove we didn't need these cards, but I'm really worried that we're working at odds instead of working together. I thought you two might have some words of wisdom for me."

After a little conversation and a lot of listening, Kyra, Michelle, and Tom arrive at a conclusion. The top managers had talked about reengineering the time-control reporting system and, in the spirit of empowerment, had asked the engineers for their suggestions. Then nothing happened.... The engineers thought their suggestions would be implemented because their managers had said to them, "You'll tell us how we should do this rather than us imposing it on you." Then top management didn't listen. Kyra was trying to figure out the message these managers were sending to the engineers.

What answers did Tom and Michelle offer Kyra? Listen in with us.

"Maybe the best approach is to be honest with the engineers," Michelle recommends. "Explain that the creation of an empowering organization is still new to us too and that we're all part of a learning process."

"And I'd suggest that you work together to define what each person or group is actually responsible for in the organization," Tom adds. "That should help clarify the boundaries and expectations for their recommendations—and the corresponding response from top management—in the future."

"That makes sense to me," Kyra replies. "I know from our training that *saying* you're going to be empowered doesn't necessarily make it so. Now I've experienced that fact firsthand, and frankly I can't blame these folks for reacting the way they did. I guess it's going to be a longer, slower process than any of us expected."

"That's true of many parts of the process," Tom interjects. "But in some ways, you may find that the results are immediate. I suspect that the engineers will listen to your explanation and react immediately—and positively."

Kyra is disappointed because developing an empowering organization is going to be a longer, slower process than expected. But longer and slower is not necessarily a bad thing. In fact, it can be good. Why? Because a longer and slower process can give you longer-lasting results and faster acceptance as the organization evolves and employees gain more responsibility and authority over the work they do. In order to build trust, resiliency, and enthusiasm, you've got to take empowerment one step at a time. Just as you can't reengineer a process overnight, you can't we-engineer without establishing realistic expectations.

Rethinking change and the people and processes it affects can lead to reengineering. Rethinking and reengineering can renew relationships—if you structure them in caring, respectful ways.

> ### Instituting Change
> **Smart Managing** Whenever you institute a change, it's important to listen to the people who will be affected by that change. Help those people be responsible for suggesting changes that will help them perform better. Then help them figure out the best way to implement that change. You can be sure that those affected will then buy into it and help make sure it is a success.

## Transaction, Transition, Transformation

Traditionally, workforce–management relationships have been structured as *transactive* relationships—ones in which there's a trade or exchange of one bit of power for another, of one level of performance for another. Empowering workforce–management relationships are structured as *transformative* in nature—ones in which power is created, in which responsibilities increase, and in which performance continuously improves.

What comes between *transactive* and *transformative* relationships? *Transition.* Transition is the process of moving from individual goals, concerns, and changes to organizational goals, concerns, and changes. Structuring that transition requires changing reporting relationships and team relationships. Implementing that transition requires *participative management.* So that's our next focus.

Creating participative management requires you to take five steps:

1. Develop leadership skills that show your belief in people and your commitment to excellence. Entrust the employees with significant, increasing responsibility and aim for significant, ongoing performance improvement. (Key word: *significant.*)
2. Build teamwork skills and valuing skills (as discussed in Chapter 6). Accept individual differences, build trust, foster leadership skills in others, and strengthen group communication and decision making. (Key word: *valuing.*)
3. Create strategic vision (more about this in Chapter 9) from the ground up. Involve all the stakeholders in the visioning process, and support the vision energetically. (Key word: *vision.*)
4. Ensure that your behavior and your words are congruent. (In other words, put your money where your mouth is.) Stabilize your relationships with personnel policies that include employee surveys and input, fair and competitive reward systems and job placements, and growth-oriented performance-evaluation processes (see Chapter 10). (Key word: *congruent.*)
5. Flatten the hierarchy, broaden employee span of control and freedom, and be systematic and inclusive about planning, budgeting, and resourcing. (Remember, we said structuring can't be accidental or haphazard.) Create a participative, dynamic—not restrictive—environment. (Key word: *inclusive.*)

When you structure transition with participative management, you reinforce and enhance the empowering characteristics of your relationships: significance, value, vision, congruence, and inclusion.

And you're left with *transformation*.

## You Are What You Implement

While you're trying to reengineer your organization into one that empowers employees, it's logical to expect that there will be some pitfalls in this process. If you can avoid those pitfalls, you can definitely say you're on the way to *we*-engineering.

In the book *Reengineering the Corporation*, Michael Hammer and James Champy, outline reasons why reengineering efforts sometimes fail. Here are some of the significant ones:

- Resistance to change (which, you'll remember, can be overcome by involving others and yourself in the change, not announcing it after the fact).
- Unrealistic expectations (which you can overcome by clearly stating areas of responsibility).
- Late staff involvement (which you can overcome with participative management).
- Lack of team skills (which you can overcome by improving group communication and leadership qualities, by investing in training).
- Lack of executive consensus (which you can overcome by creating a congruent, strategic vision).

## Structured Design: Feng Shui and Ergonomics

Have you heard of *feng shui* and been curious enough to find out more? It's a Chinese concept that has to do with creating harmony in your environment. It's a useful metaphor for understanding how physical surroundings shape the work experience of everyone in the organization as well as that of customers. From architecture to artwork, from decorating to ergonomics, the environment in which you and your employees work can be debilitating or uplifting, can waste value or inspire productivity. (For more, check out the Centre for Feng Shui Research Web site, www.geomancy.net.)

Not only that, but the environment in which you and your employees work can cost you money or save you money. What's the return on investment for an ergonomic workstation, for example, compared with the drain of a lawsuit or long-term health care for an employee with repetitive-motion injury? As a leader in an empowering organization, shouldn't part of your leadership activities be directed at structuring a safe, sane, and comfortable workplace?

The point here is to manage the entire *milieu*— the physical, emotional, social, and cultural settings and interactions that make up the workplace—to maximize an empowering environment.

> **Key Term**
>
> **Feng Shui** The ancient Chinese practice of arranging a physical environment to maximize balanced energy, or *chi*, in the belief that if an environment has good *chi*, its inhabitants will be healthy.
>
> Although it's relatively new to the U.S., *feng shui* (pronounced *fung shway*) has been around for centuries. In Chinese, the term means "wind and water." The practice of *feng shui* in the West seeks to harmonize the layout and orientation of both home and workplace. Energy flow is a critical element, as is the concept of *yin* and *yang*, complementary forces that contribute to balance in your surroundings.

## Ergonomic or Injurious?

Let's look first at the ergonomics issue. Here are some numbers to give you some idea of the impact that repetitive motion, lifting, pushing, or pulling—ergonomic injuries—have in today's workplace. Just read this passage from the proposal by the Occupational Safety and Health Administration to amend Part 1910 of title 29 of the Code of Federal Regulations (November 1999):

> Work-related musculoskeletal disorders (MSDs) currently account for one-third of all occupational injuries and illnesses

reported to the Bureau of Labor Statistics (BLS) by employers every year. These disorders thus constitute the largest job-related injury and illness problem in the United States today. In 1997, employers reported a total of 626,000 lost workday MSDs to the BLS, and these disorders accounted for $1 of every $3 spent for workers' compensation in that year. Employers pay more than $15-$20 billion in workers' compensation costs for these disorders every year, and other expenses associated with MSDs may increase this total to $45-$54 billion a year. Workers with severe MSDs can face permanent disability that prevents them from returning to their jobs or handling simple, everyday tasks.

**Key Term** **Ergonomic** Applying the principles of *ergonomics*, the science of learning about human abilities and limitations, and using that knowledge to improve people's interaction with tools, systems, and their environment. If you want to design a workplace that's *ergonomic*, you'll need to account for the needs, capabilities, and capacities of employees in equipment, furnishings, and surroundings. If you design—or structure—an ergonomic environment, the payoffs will be enormous in terms of comfort, safety, and dollars.

Can your organization afford its share of these costs? On the other hand, what could your organization do with the savings from preventing ergonomic injuries? Let's say that one employee develops carpal tunnel syndrome, which health professionals assure you is the direct result of years of repetitive keyboarding. Let's say the required surgery and recovery means that the employee will be either out of the office entirely or in the office but not performing normally for three months. During that three months, you're paying the employee's salary and benefits *and* you're paying for temporary help and training time for the temporary help and extra supervision for the temporary help and increased concern on the part of other employees who may have some of the same symptoms and.... Well, you get the picture!

The costs you accumulate during an episode like this are not, then, just monetary—although those costs alone can be staggering. The costs bleed into the quality of the workplace experience for everyone, they drain morale, and they alienate workers and customers alike.

What do you do? How can you save money and morale in an empowering way? How do you create an empowering milieu? First of all, you should take a proactive stance. Make an ergonomic environment, in the office or the shop, a priority. It shows you care about your employees, and it also helps people become more productive—two positive outcomes. And if you don't know what ergonomics issues exist in your workplace, find out.

**Don't Wait**

Don't wait for government regulations or lawsuits to force you to show that you care for your employees. What message will you send if you wait until someone's injured to take action?

Although you can't expect to anticipate every possible injury or discomfort, you can structure an environment that's healthier, safer, and user-friendlier. Doing so reaps rewards by echoing that your actions are as empowering as your talk. (It's the *congruence* piece of empowerment.)

1. Don't leave anyone—or any place—out. It's not just the shop floor or computer centers where workplace injuries can occur.
2. Don't feel as though you have to reinvent the wheel. Talk with other professionals in other organizations who've put preventive measures in place.
3. Don't ignore the demographics of the workforce. Just knowing the ages of the people you work with will give you lots of data.
4. Don't rely on the results of one study or one report. Remember that information comes fast and furious in the medical field; the latest study is not necessarily the most indicative.
5. Don't forget the bottom line. Although not everyone will buy into the empowering principles that you've adopted, no one can argue with the monetary impact of *not* dealing with ergonomics.

## It Takes All Kinds

As the saying goes, it take all kinds to make a world. And even in the micro world of your workplace, you're not likely to find consensus on the best look and feel for that environment. There's probably no office in the world where everyone is comfortable with a given room temperature. Certainly it's unlikely that any two of us would see eye to eye on the appeal of a particular artist's work. Just stroll around from office to office or from cubicle to cubicle and you'll notice how much people differ in their ideas about design and decor. You won't be able to please everyone.

So maybe trying to add esthetic value to the workplace is not the safest highway to empowerment. But you can safely navigate some side roads—if you gather and share information and responsibility, if you invest in learning and planning, if you use esthetics to reinforce your company's spirit and relationships. Try asking your employees these questions:

- How's the light in your space? Does it add esthetic value to your workplace or does it anesthetize all those who enter? Changes can be inexpensive and dramatic: changing bulb strength, making the lighting adjustable, adding or taking away lamps or light fixtures, redirecting light beams.

### Color or Black-and-White?

What seems like a little thing can mean a lot. In one several-story-high office building we know of, management assigned one individual to choose the wall color for the entire building. She completed her assignment, single-handedly, and announced her choice.

One little decision created a lot of havoc. Everyone had their own ideas about wall color, it turns out, and almost no one liked hers. (As an interior decorator friend of ours says, "It never ceases to amaze me how differently people see the same color.") So she relinquished the unilateral decision-making for shared decision-making. The members of each department decided on their own wall color—and harmony was restored.

- Does your parking space say something about how much the organization values you? Are closer spaces reserved for those "higher up" in the organization? One company's employee survey revealed that those with reserved parking spaces farthest from the building entrance were most unhappy with the parking system. The result? No assigned spaces, happier employees.
- What does the size of your office say about how you work? In an organization that's empowering, do the old trappings of "success"—corner office with a view and a wet bar—still fit? On a more practical note, does the size of your office fit the time you spend there? If you spend more time in team or group efforts, can your individual space be reduced and your communal space be increased?
- Is your office building respectful of—or, one step further, a credit to—the neighborhood it occupies? Does it show the spirit of your organization? Does it display the care you take to consider employee and customer needs and values?
- Can your organization offer benefits that add value to employees' lives? As part of a stress-reduction drive at Charles Schwab, for example, on-site dry cleaning and take-home meals from the cafeteria reduced absenteeism.
- How does dress affect your workplace? Not everyone or every company is up to "casual Fridays" or "whatever turns you on" dress codes. But you might be interested— and surprised—to hear others' opinions and ideas about dress. Some companies, for example, have found that uniforms (if no more than an agreement to wear khakis and navy shirts) make it easier and less expensive for their employees to come to work: no "What-do-I-wear-today?" choices.

We can't know what innovations you'll make or what other esthetics you'll address—the flow of air and energy, the composition or placement of furnishings, the use of artwork, for example.

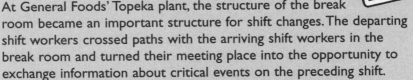

### Structuring the "We"

How can physical surroundings be part of we-engineering? At General Foods' Topeka plant, the structure of the break room became an important structure for shift changes. The departing shift workers crossed paths with the arriving shift workers in the break room and turned their meeting place into the opportunity to exchange information about critical events on the preceding shift.

A small but significant object made these spontaneous meetings routine—and valuable: an always-full coffee pot. That simple device served a vital role in we-engineering the process of transferring information between shifts.

We can be sure that you're now better prepared to build the future by structuring your surroundings, setting the stage, choreographing the dance of empowerment.

## Manager's Checklist for Chapter 7

❑ Consciously and conscientiously—not accidentally or haphazardly—design, construct, and use organizational space and relationships to empower your organization.

❑ Rethink and reengineer to renew, focusing on relationships not just on processes.

❑ Convert transactive relationships into transformative ones with transitions that use participative management.

❑ Consider esthetics and ergonomics to structure space. Evaluate how your workplace space affects your attitudes, meets or opposes your needs, fuels your creativity or stifles your ingenuity. Find out how others perceive their office space, and together do what you can to improve your environment. Remember the concept of *kaizen*, continuous improvement? Do what you can, a little at a time, but always in the direction of structuring it better.

# Empowering Employees: The Magic of Response-Ability

*The actuality of thought is life.*
—Aristotle, *Metaphysics*

It's Sunday morning. You're reading the newspaper over a cup of coffee. You flip pages. The next section is the want ads. You scan a few. "Seeking enthusiastic, motivated individuals who want to make their highest goals a reality," says one. "Dedicated to delivering world-class service by helping our clients and our people excel," touts another. "Must be able to maintain a high level of morale in a diverse workforce," says the next one.

What, you wonder, can I do to help create employees who are enthusiastic and motivated, who set high goals and make them real, who deliver world-class service, who ensure high morale and support diversity?

Well, pour another cup of coffee. We're about to find out what makes people love their jobs (or not), what kind of environment contributes to that, what the difference is between

**Actualize** To make real by turning into action, according to the general definition in the dictionary. In empowering terms, *actualize* refers to the coming together of all the building blocks of empowerment as the spirit in which the individual performs at a high level the work he or she is best prepared to do.

motivation and liberation, and how responsibility enables response-ability.

In other words, we're going to talk about what makes for an *actualizing* organizational experience. Creating such an experience is the next step in building an empowering organization.

## I Love My Job—or Do I?

"I've been noticing two of our team members' behavior lately," Tom is telling Michelle, "and how differently they respond to performing the same tasks.

"I wasn't really getting anywhere in trying to understand the differences, though, until I decided to just ask them how they felt about coming to work. What they said opened my eyes.

"Susan, who's always upbeat, ready for a challenge, and eager for more responsibility, described herself as hopping out of bed in the morning already loaded with anticipation about the exciting things she'll get to do at work. Phil—after much coaxing to overcome his reticence—described himself as having a hard time getting started each day, as constantly watching the clock, as never feeling truly part of the team."

"Sounds like we need to explore these differences further," Michelle suggests. "Can we pinpoint what makes Susan love her job and Phil seem to dread it?"

Could you explain these differences among your employees? (Or in yourself, for that matter?)

In late 1995, *Inc.* magazine enlisted Gallup to help survey workers, to find out how they felt about their jobs. You might be pleasantly surprised by the results (reported by Jeffrey L. Seglin, "The Happiest Workers in the World," *Inc.,* May 15, 1996). Roughly 70% of U.S. workers reported they were satisfied with their jobs. There's more:

- 87% said the company's *mission* made them feel important.
- 84% felt their jobs offered opportunities for *learning* and *growth*.
- 82% felt they were given the chance to *do their best* every day.
- 72% felt that someone at work *encouraged* their development.
- 70% felt their managers helped make the company a *great place to work*.
- 69% felt they were *fairly compensated*.

Two years later, a second survey (Jeffrey L. Seglin, "The 1998 *Inc.*/Gallup Survey: Americans @ Work," *Inc.*, June 1, 1998) produced similar results—and also reported that a whopping 96% of the workers surveyed said they *know what's expected of them* at work.

Beginning to get some clues to what makes people love their jobs? Let's explore further—from the other side of the fence, the perspective of that 30% who are not satisfied with their jobs.

---

### Tell 'Em What to Expect

Here's the situation: Cole leaves his consulting job to take a job teaching software. He's a skilled, certified trainer in several software programs and has years of experience.

Instead of developing and delivering training programs, instead of working in the community to build clientele, instead of using his specialized skills—all the things he thought he'd be doing—he finds that his employer expects him first to sell software, then to teach it if there's time.

Is he a satisfied employee? Does he feel he has the opportunity to do his best every day? Does he believe he has the opportunity to learn and grow?

If you want to recruit—and, more important, keep—talented workers, tell them what to expect up front. You'll be doing the right thing that way: for the employee, the organization, and yourself.

### Why the Spirit Doesn't Move Them

What is it that makes people "burn out" on the job? What frustrations cause them to leave or at least to distance themselves from their fellow employees? Here are a few factors:

- **Boredom.** Work days seem too long; people have to do the same tasks too many times.
- **Overwork.** People work too long over too long a period of time; frustration and fatigue ensue.
- **Not enough work.** People don't feel needed; their work seems menial or meaningless.
- **Poor relationships at the office.** Strained relations with other workers cause a loss of interest; feelings of hopelessness set in.

If you've ever been dissatisfied with a job, you can probably name a few more factors. People can and will articulate what's satisfying and what's dissatisfying about their jobs—but you've got to ask them.

When you ask, you may find that people who love their jobs say things like:

> **Smart Managing**
> ### Doing Something About It
> It's not unusual for employees not to admit they're unhappy with their jobs. If they do so, it's uncertain whether they might be transferred or even invited to leave. As an empowering manager, you'll need to risk finding out whether the employees around you are happy or unhappy with their jobs. If they're unhappy, it affects their performance (and yours). If you can find out what's troubling them, you can do something about it by using the information you have to foster better matches between jobs and individuals.

- My manager respects me. (And not surprisingly, these folks respect their managers in return.)
- I'm recognized for what I do well. (And these folks recognize the contributions of others.)
- I feel that the people I work with care about me. (And that care is mutual.)
- I have the tools I need to do my job. (And these people act as resources for others.)

- My company supports my involvement with my family and in my community. (And these workers support the organization when it gets involved in community activities.)
- The people I work with are committed to high performance. (And this fosters commitment on the part of the employee.)

Notice that these statements have to do with feelings, with relationships, with the capacity and the capability to perform well. Here's the key: empowered employees—you're included here, you know—are motivated, self-directing, and self-actualizing.

As an empowering manager, your job is not to motivate others. Only they can do that. (Employees aren't machines with "M" buttons you can push!) Your job is to work with others to promote the liberating conditions that permeate the organization. Your job is to help people find the work they love and learn to love the work they do best.

> **Motivation** What incites, impels, induces someone to act in a certain way. That's the literal definition. Taken in terms of empowering, the meaning of motivation goes a little deeper.
>
> The strongest *motivation* is intrinsic: the reward comes from the process, the experience of *doing* the job. Extrinsic rewards—the *getting* part of the experience—are far less motivating in the long run. The difference, as Steven Berglas puts it in his article, "When Money Talks, People Walk" (*Inc.*, May 1, 1996), is between "psychological commitment" and "purchased compliance."

## Keepers and Finders

If people *are* the organization and if satisfied people help *create* an empowered organization, how do you foster the kind of satisfaction that brings about empowerment? One way is to reverse the old "finders keepers" adage and play "keepers finders" instead. As with any game, there are rules, but you can add your own after you've become an experienced player. We'll call this "match play" because we'll match the rules to the reasons people love their jobs.

**Rule One:** Ensure that the company's mission is reinforced, reiterated, and reinvigorated with each effort, each task, each project. How do you do this—and make people feel their jobs are important in the process? If employees don't have a clear, personal vision, they can't connect their own goals with the company's goals. If they can't make that personal connection, they can't take personal responsibility for the company's success.

**Rule Two:** Offer employees opportunities to stretch, learn, and grow. Employment security is out; employability is in. What we yearn for is the chance to create our own personal *kaizen*, or continuous improvement, of our knowledge, skills, and personal and professional growth. Give workers the opportunity to learn and grow, and you'll get empowered employees. Help employees identify training opportunities they want and need. Ask the newly trained to train someone else. You'll build bonds among people, increase leadership opportunities, and develop confident, actualizing workers.

**Rule Three:** Make it possible for everyone to perform to their fullest capacity and capability, every day. Sound like a tall order? Take a step at a time. Take a temperature reading every morning: notice whether individuals are high or low on energy—and find out why. Measure the barometric pressure in relationships: if pressure is high between two employees, create ways to lower the tension. Test the waters for comfort with physical surroundings: if noise levels are too high, for example, brainstorm how to overcome or eliminate the static. Check for operational comfort, too: purposeful meetings, timeliness, meaningful reporting requirements. Provide the resources that employees need to perform well. Better yet, know your employees well enough to anticipate their needs.

**Rule Four:** Offer genuine encouragement, not faint praise. Prerequisite: know your employees on more than a superficial level. What untapped talent lurks beneath the surface, one that you can encourage by recognizing it? Who's a little reticent about their expertise, and how can you help them shine? Who's exhausted every skill upgrade in a particular area, and how can you create opportunities for them to try something new?

Implementing these "rules" will help you—together with your employees—make the workplace a great place to be.

If you match people, their skills, interests, dreams, talents, and goals with jobs that help them stretch, reach, enhance, fulfill, build, and attain, you'll have passed another milepost on the road to empowerment. You'll create an organization that *keeps* its valuable members, and you'll create an organization that *finds* members who add value.

## Seek and You Shall Find

In the perfectly empowered organization (an impossibility, since empowerment is not a state but a journey), turnover would be very low. Even if it were possible to have perfectly happy employees all the time, some are bound to want to retire, some are bound to move to another area because their spouse has accepted a new position, some are bound to have children or elderly parents that they have to care for, and some may just find opportunities they can't pass up.

So at some point, you're going to have to seek out new talent. We thought you might find these examples* revealing—and inspiring.

Select Comfort, a mattress manufacturer, recruits by postcard from among its customers. The company hired one

> ### Cost of Losses
>
> Sometimes we lose sight of the fact that the loss of a skilled employee doesn't just make it difficult to complete a project or respond to a customer or achieve a difficult goal. It also costs money. "Because replacing an employee costs approximately three times his or her wages in lost productivity, training, and recruiting costs, people mistakes *are* financial mistakes," says Donna Fenn.* Recognize how much turnover costs, then, in both human and monetary terms—and work a little every day to reduce the reasons for it.

*Donna Fenn, "The Right Fit," *Inc.*, October 15, 1997.

**Diversity in Age**

**Smart Managing** Are all your employees pretty similar in age? If so, consider diversifying your workforce by recruiting across the age barrier. What does age diversification bring to the workplace? Perspective, for one thing, on business cycles, on continuity, on values, on experience.

customer—with no prior retail experience—to manage a new store, and she exceeded sales goals in 11 out of 12 months. Her secret? She believed the company's mattress had saved her husband from back surgery, and she conveyed that enthusiasm to other customers. Her beliefs and goals were aligned with the beliefs and mission of the organization.

The same company looks for employees in other types of retail outlets, such as electronics or furniture stores. Their theory? If you attract talent from diverse backgrounds, you'll get diverse experience and skills.

Current employees can be good resources for recruiting new employees, and some companies offer incentives for referrals. But whether referring employees receive an incentive or not, they tend to refer others who are a good fit for the organization; they typically take the referral process seriously. After all, no one wants to be associated with a poor performer.

Sometimes employee referrals are "all in the family." At Betek Manufacturing, for example, 30% of employees are related to other employees. The family ties make work life easier in several ways: similar values, the ability to train each other, carpooling, and sharing information inside and outside the workplace, formally and informally.

Some companies recruit employees based on the work environment's structure—or the flexibility of its structure. Neverdahl-Loft & Associates, a computer consulting firm, promotes the fact that workers don't have to be local: 93 of 100 employees work away from the firm's main office.

In our experience, some companies develop close recruiting-oriented relationships, like Shell Oil and the University of West Florida, for example. The company has learned over the years that the university turns out many students who fit into the company culture and who perform well in that environment—so the organization consistently and frequently recruits among UWF's students.

Contract employees or consultants can be valuable additions to your workforce, too. They're familiar with your values, they understand your mission, they're experienced at working with your employees, and they have proven skills that add value to your product or service.

---

### Quick Checklist: Empowered Employees

How empowered are your employees? In an article for *Organizational Dynamics* ("Seven Questions Every Leader Should Consider," Autumn 1997), Robert Quinn and Gretchen Spreitzer list these characteristics that empowered employees have in common:

- Self-determination, the freedom to decide how to do their jobs.
- A sense of meaning, that their work matters and that they care about it.
- A sense of competence, that they're able to do their jobs well.
- A sense of impact, that they can make a difference and that others listen to them.

---

## The Value of Money in an Empowered Organization

Successfully recruiting and retaining valued employees involves not only matching talent and tasks, but also money (unless you're working entirely with volunteers). We hope by now that you've grasped the concept that liberating, actualizing organizations build in those intrinsic motivators that people are hungry for, that enable them to perform highly, that make work a part of their lives instead of just a place they go.

But they've also got to be compensated monetarily.

How meaningful is money? When we frequently hear that people are trying to balance "getting ahead" in the office with "getting a life" outside the office, is any amount of money enough compensation? Can you pay someone enough to work 60

## Model What You Value

In a recent interview (Reed Abelson, "A Leader's-Eye View of Leadership," *The New York Times*, October 10, 1999), Shelly Lazarus, chairman and chief executive of ad agency Ogilvy & Mather Worldwide, said, "When I stay out for three months for maternity leave, I am well aware that that makes it all right to take maternity leave.

"And if the CEO isn't going to the school play, ... is canceling his vacation, ... is not coming home to be at his 6-year-old's birthday party, well then, the rest of the company knows how they're supposed to behave."

Lazarus is well aware of how her values and behavior set standards for the workforce. What standards do your values and behavior set?

hours in a week, to forgo their children's ball games or dance recitals, to eat on the run, to interrupt or postpone vacations to get an important project done?

## Work as Addiction

Be careful not to send the message like this. "Wanna be Wonderwoman [or Superman]? You too can work 80-hour weeks, jog 5 miles each day, serve as Scout master for your child's troop, take work home every weekend, win the Employee of the Month award six times a year ...." Instead of creating Wonderwoman or Superman, however, such messages encourage workaholism—as addicting as drugs or alcohol for some of us. According to Anne Wilson Schaef and Diane Fassel in *The Addictive Organization*, "It is the actual *process of working* that is the fix, not the outcome. Like any addiction, work takes over one's life, it becomes primary, resulting in a loss of perspective on other realities." Be careful.

Oh, maybe a large paycheck will cause some employees to work longer hours to finish a last-minute project, to sacrifice the health and social benefits of eating well, to justify missing an important family event. Maybe it will move some employees who lack internal initiative, but will it move them for the next project and the one after that if money is the only reward?

Is this the kind of behavior an empowering organization wants to reinforce? You know better! That large paycheck won't improve the quality of life for the things that really count, for the relationships that matter, or ultimately for the values and qualities your organization holds dear.

How can you add value to compensation—monetary or other—in ways that reinforce an empowering culture? One way to do so is to build a system that doesn't confine compensation to movement up a career ladder, to a change in title, or to an increase in workload. Build a system that promotes team effort with cross-department communication. Build a system that allows people to explore their talents or interests, to step "outside the box." Build a system that's responsive to the intrinsic, social, and individual motivations that are inherent in the people you work with. Show appreciation for what individuals give to you and to the organization. But don't fail also to pay people at or above market level. That's only fair, and you're likely to get more than your money's worth.

So, now that you've created a system that keeps valuable employees and that finds ones who will be valuable, what have you got? You've got flexibility, diversity, reliability, creativity, the ability to develop relationships. You've created compensation that's fair *and* intrinsic. And—ahhh!—you've got employees who are eager to be responsible. Your role is to help them become response-able.

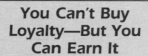

**You Can't Buy Loyalty—But You Can Earn It**

What do workers say about medical benefits, 401(k)s, tuition reimbursement, personal valet services, and pay raises? They say these perks are nice, but they don't buy loyalty.

What earns their loyalty? When the boss involves them in decisions, lets them make a mistake without humiliating them in public, gets to know the names of their spouses and children, recognizes the importance of personal and family life, and allows them a small amount of work time each week to attend to personal matters. You can't buy it. You earn it.

## Free to Be Response-Able

We all think we know what it means to be *responsible*, and often we want the people we work with to be more responsible. If

---

**⚠ CAUTION!**

### Does a Test Tell All?

Don't rely solely on a test—a personality profile, a behavior traits survey, a preference index—to make hiring decisions for you. While the indicators such "tests" provide can give you clues, don't let them lull you into labeling, jumping to conclusions, or denying opportunity.

One of the authors, years ago, was first given an extensive battery of personality and behavior tests, then interviewed at length by three managers in a training and development department. This resulted in getting hired and successfully matched to a fulfilling job. But it almost didn't happen. As one manager put it, "Your scores on one test indicated that you're pretty unfeeling when it comes to reacting in an emergency or a crisis. But, knowing that your background was in child protection casework, we realized that you'd learned to separate yourself from traumatic feelings so that you could react quickly, decisively, and logically in a crisis. And that knowledge changed the way we viewed the test results."

---

that's true, how do we enable responsibility? We work with our employees to enable *response-ability*.

**Key Term**

**Response-Ability** The ability of employees to respond to both internal and external customers in ways that contribute to personal and organizational missions, to create and innovate in ways that add value to products and services, to be *responsible* for their own contributions, and to take initiative for their own growth.

By creating a work environment that allows mistakes and encourages learning from them, that equates success less with movement up a career ladder and more with learning and growing across career possibilities, that compensates workers fairly and intrinsically, you will have enabled *response-ability*.

One way to begin creating response-ability is to consider what happens when you feel someone is irresponsible. First, examine your own behavior and your management style. (Check out the Appendix.) Next, examine what you know about the employee in question—his or her strengths, values, personality. Then, examine the situation. Instead of judging and labeling someone "irresponsible" for not doing what *you* want them to do, consider what *is* working and what *is not* working about the situation. Ask yourself why and why not. Ask whether changing your behavior will bring about change in the employee. Ask how changing the situation might transform irresponsible behavior into responsible behavior.

In other words, consider all the factors that contribute to a particular behavior. Instead of expecting employees to have "natural" responsibility, help them develop response-ability.

### Dual Career Options vs. Singular Career Ladders

Honeywell Inc. offers dual career options instead of merely the standard one-track career ladder. For some employees, the chance to participate in a science/engineering research-fellows program may be more appealing than pursuing a management track. The pay and prestige are equivalent. The difference is in the way the employee feels about the choice.

Source: "The New Meaning of Success," U.S. News & World Report, September 17, 1990, p. 58.

When you match jobs with people, when you reward them in ways that are meaningful, when you model a passion for your business life and for your private life, you're rewarded with employees who are vital, creative, and self-directing. When you combine all the preceding building blocks of empowerment—informing, leading, coaching, providing, and structuring—you'll succeed at actualizing.

## Manager's Checklist for Chapter 8

❑ Know what's satisfying and what's not about your employees' views of their workplace.

❑ Realize that motivation is not something you can impose on someone else. You can't flip a switch and turn it on. It's intrinsic.

❑ Create a keepers-finders atmosphere in which the value of both current and new talent is apparent.

❏ Attract employees whose values and beliefs align with the organization's mission.

❏ Recognize the limits of money as compensation and the unlimited value of appreciation.

❏ Build in opportunities for developing your employees, development that will yield long-term, sustainable, response-able results.

# Ask the Right Questions: From Problem Solving to High Performance

*We never know how high we are*
*Till we are called to rise.*
*And then, if we are true to plan*
*Our statures touch the skies.*
                    —Emily Dickinson

*C hange.* What images does that word conjure up for you?
Does the thought make you flush with excitement and
anticipation—or cringe with dread and fear? Do you consider
yourself ready for it, whether it feels like "biting the bullet" or
"riding the rocket?"

Truth be told, change can often be a little frightening for
many of us. It suggests the unknown, and we're not sure we'll
be able to adapt successfully. Creating an empowering organization can involve a lot of change, but it doesn't have to be a
cause of anxiety and uncertainty if it's informed and well-
planned. You now have the building blocks you need, and
you're ready to implement the actions that will build an

empowering organization and result in higher performance throughout your organization.

So, let's find strength in what we know together and brave the unknown. Let's bring that change process out of the dark and into the light of day. That way, it won't be nearly so uncertain—and it will take us somewhere we want to go: to lasting high performance.

## Benchmarking for High Performance

Benchmarking. You may have done it yourself. You may have read about other companies doing it. But what will it mean for you on the journey to empowerment? How can you use it to develop a change-ready, actualized organization?

Benchmarks indicate ways of behaving, producing, or achieving. They are indicators of high performance, often performance you want to emulate. Often they come from a competitor. Sometimes they're shared openly and reported in the press or in company publications.

**Benchmark** A measurement of performance, also called *best practice* or *exemplary practice*, often a practice that's been developed or perfected by one of your competitors. Depending on the business you're in, that measurement may be one (or more) of a process, a procedure, a method, a technique, or an approach. Regardless of the type of measurement, a benchmark is an indicator of high performance—and perhaps an indicator of a change you want to make in your own organization.

Suppose you're in manufacturing and you admire the sales technique of one of your foreign competitors. The competitor's approach to fielding salespeople worldwide has been widely studied and reported. You think you have a pretty good understanding of the competitor's methods and you decide to implement them.

Six months later, your implementation has fallen flat. You're befuddled and frustrated—and so is everyone on the sales team. What went wrong?

Maybe your "pretty good understanding" suffered from a lack of information. Maybe you did a pretty good job of studying the other organization. But maybe you didn't do enough studying of your own organization. So the change you tried to implement in your organization was poorly implemented and didn't get the results you were hoping for.

Knowing what other organizations are doing successfully is a very small part of effecting change. Knowing how such change will play out at home is a very big part.

So, have a plan for change. Don't assume that someone else's system will fit your environment or be embraced enthusiastically by your employees. And before you develop an implementation plan, ask yourself—and your employees—questions like these:

- How does our culture compare with the benchmark organization's? What similarities are there? What are the differences?
- Do we really know what it is we do now? Can we measure it? If not, how will we know what effects the change will have?
- How embedded are our existing systems? What will we keep? What will we eliminate?
- What specific changes will we make? What's the timetable?
- Will we welcome changes to our processes and procedures? How will such changes affect individuals, in terms of both feelings and performance?
- Will some individuals sabotage change—intentionally or unintentionally? If so, what can we do to overcome such behaviors?
- Can we accept that a competitor's methodology is better than ours? Will the changes fit our values?
- Will we adjust compensation systems, information systems, communication systems as needed?
- Do we have commitment at all levels of the organization, across departments, within teams?

- Have we established a measurement system to track progress and evaluate certain milestones that let us know where we stand?
- Are we flexible enough to make adjustments as we go along?
- How will change lead us to high performance? In other words, what are our expectations?

---

### Planning for Change

In the mid-'90s, a failing Continental Airlines studied and adopted Southwest Airlines' cross-utilization process, using the same person to handle baggage and take tickets, for example. When employees grumbled about having more work to do, Continental struck a deal: employees listed all the useless or redundant things they did each day, and the company reduced or eliminated them.

The result: less resistance to change and more acceptance of the cross-utilization approach.

Source: C. H. Deutsch, "Competitors Can Teach You a Lot, but the Lessons Can Hurt," *The New York Times*, July 18, 1999, p. BU4.

---

One more thing about benchmarking. Why do you imagine that successful organizations essentially give away their secrets of success? Aren't they afraid of what their competitors will achieve on the basis of such information? The answer is "probably not." They're not worried because most of their competitors will be so busy copying their techniques that they'll forget to consider their own culture, people, and commitment to change.

Now that you know how to succeed after benchmarking, you won't forget those factors that make a crucial difference, will you?

You can't expect to take benchmarks or best practices at face value. Your culture may not match that of the benchmark organization; your systems may not have evolved in the same ways; your mission may differ. If you look only at an organization's procedures, you'll miss the point. Look deeper, at the other, people-oriented factors that contribute to high performance. Then plan your own changes by adjusting for the attitudes, skills, and goals of the people in your organization.

## The Performance of a Lifetime

Michelle runs into Tom in the hallway. "I overheard a supervisor in accounting today tell an employee, 'I don't care what the reason is, if you don't finish this by tomorrow morning, I'll withdraw my recommendation for your promotion.'" She pauses. "Boy, that sounded harsh."

> ### High Performance
>
> If you want to define *high performance*, you'll have to use words with lots of "-bility": flexibility, adaptability, credibility, responsibility. And lots of "-ity": integrity, vitality, quality. High performance results from the convergence of all the building blocks of empowerment in an organization where people have authority and responsibility for their work and who work well with fellow employees to continuously improve processes.

"You're not kidding," Tom replies. "Wonder what he thought he'd accomplish by threatening an employee?"

We wonder too. While you're in the process of analyzing and planning for change to an empowering organization, ponder this: What creates positive and proactive energy in your organization? Is it a threat—like the loss of a promotion? Is it the threat of reduced market share? Is it the threat of a competitor's new product beating yours to market? Is it the threat of downsizing or reorganizing?

If the energy in your organization results from threats—whatever form they take—it's probably mostly *reactive* and short-lived. When the threat dissipates, the energy dissipates along with it.

In *The Philanthropic Quest*, James Gregory Lord identifies other energy sources that can fizzle out just as quickly:

* Maybe the energy in your organization emanates from a crisis, a problem, a "situation." You might mark down merchandise to increase sales, increase your advertising budget to boost brand name awareness, or hire temporaries to shore up your workforce—but when the crisis passes, when the "problem" is solved, the energy slips out the door with it.

- Perhaps your organization puts its energy into maintaining the status quo. If so, energy gets sapped by dealing with everyday, mundane "to-do lists"—and there's none left to devote to a vision of the organization's future.
- Maybe the status quo isn't acceptable in your organization, and your energy is ignited from wanting more: more profit, more customers, more products, more .... We think you'll find yourself squinting, because your goals are shortsighted, and you're energizing on the basis of quantity, not quality.

If your energy has nowhere to go, that's exactly where it goes: nowhere. When your energy derives from problems or threats, it peaks, then it hits bottom. It flows in sharp points instead of smooth transitions. Instead of continuous improvement, you get discontinuous correction.

So what do you do? You adjust your outlook, your focus, your direction. You become more forward-thinking, more quality-oriented, more opportunity-seeking. You change in a planned, organized, learning mode. You become proactive rather than just reactive.

## Get a Life: Strike a Balance

Let's talk attitude—and change. Say someone driving parallel to you begins to move into your lane. Do you bang your palm on the steering wheel, lay on your horn, and utter words that you'd normally not use in polite company? Or do you understand that we all make mistakes, sound your horn long enough to warn the other driver, and assume that he or she didn't really set out to sideswipe you?

In business as in life, if you expect something to happen a certain way, it often does. If you assume an attitude in someone else, that attitude is what you project on someone else. If you fly off the handle, you may provoke the same behavior in your target. If you treat others with understanding and respect, they're more likely to treat you the same way.

> ### ⚠️ CAUTION!
> ### The Halo Effect
> Expectations can set us up to achieve, they can color our attitudes, and they can make reality of visions. But they can also mislead, particularly if we overgeneralize on the basis of our expectations, creating "a potential inaccuracy in estimation or judgment," which is the dictionary definition of *halo effect.*
>
> In *The Thin Book of Appreciative Inquiry,* Sue Annis Hammond defines *halo effect* by example: a high-IQ student's behavior is labeled "creative" when the same behavior in a low-IQ student might be labeled "destructive," or similar performances are labeled "high" or "low" depending on whether the individual in question is perceived as generally high-performing or low-performing.
>
> Be careful that your expectations don't cause misperceptions.

We're talking about balance, in a sense. It's easy for us to let our lives get out of balance. It's easy to fall into the habit of dealing only with today's issues, to check them off our list before we go home from the office. It's easy to forget what lies beyond today, to lose sight of the future and the actions we need to take to ensure its success. It's easy to react in familiar, habitual ways rather than in innovative, empowering ways.

But we can tip the scales so that our day-to-day habits become balanced with long-term goals. To do that, we must realize, as James Gregory Lord points out in *The Philanthropic Quest,* that "We can create what we *want.* And the very act of envisioning it may make things that were unthinkable yesterday thinkable today." In other words, we can change in nonthreatening, solution-seeking ways. We can, as Lord puts it, thrive—not just survive.

There are two key words here: *envision* and *thrive.* Remember the first time you wanted to ask your manager for increased staff, for the OK to spend money on training, for a piece of equipment, or _____ (you fill in the blank)? If you're like a lot of us, you

> **Key Term**
> **Envision** To picture something in your mind. If you want to create what you want, need, or desire, *envision* it. You may be surprised at what you can accomplish once you've pictured an event, an outcome, or an approach.

**Visualizing Achievement**

Chances are that if you take downhill skiing lessons, for example, you'll be taught to visualize every turn on a slalom course—so you can be prepared with a successful "picture" of your trip down the course.

Likewise, if you prepare for a speech, you can use visualization to practice. Picture yourself in the room, walking to the podium, placing your notes, and smiling at the audience. Feel yourself take a deep breath, hear yourself give the introduction, and picture the audience smiling back at you. In your mind, listen to how well you emphasize key points. Envision how you meet the eyes of each individual in the room. Grin as the applause begins, and watch yourself exit the stage gracefully and graciously.

Visualization can help you by allowing you to anticipate and mentally go through steps involved in success.

rehearsed your "proposal"—and that required you to envision what would take place. You imagined what you would say, what the manager would say, how it would all turn out. You created a picture in your mind (a positive one, we hope). You visualized the experience.

> **Thrive** To prosper, succeed, flourish, grow, develop. Visualize an organization that is built to grow and last and you'll visualize an organization that *thrives*. That's a company where everyone understands customer needs and wants and is organized to work together to help deliver the goods.

Visualization is not a new technique. We're probably most familiar with the term in sports. Athletes, professional and amateur, use visualization to help them go beyond their usual performance.

As for our second key word, *thrive*—it's pretty simple. You just can't thrive without envisioning processes, visualizing outcomes, and creating a shared vision.

Now that you've skewed your focus in the direction of the future with visualization, we'd like to help you achieve a little more balance. You'll need something to balance that creative thinking with reality. You'll need to know how to reach that visualized future.

## Food for the Soul of an Organization: Appreciative Inquiry

The vision you create isn't enough to get you to where you want to go. So here's another benchmark for you: *appreciative inquiry*. It's an attitude more than a technique and an outlook more than a procedure. But it's a benchmark nevertheless.

Without a vision, what have you got? Today—but no tomorrow. Without a shared vision, what have you got? The feeling that "it's us versus them" and that "things are done to us" instead of "we choose to take this action or behave this way."

Well, then, how do you overcome the "us vs. them" mentality? How do you create a vision that's shared and meaningful, not just one that's posted on the bulletin board or printed on letterhead? You can start by *listening* with genuine interest to all your *customers*.

Who are all your customers? Let's consider a few examples.

If you're part of a government agency, your customers may be the people affected by the regulations you're charged to enforce and maybe some of the members of your own agency.

> **Appreciative inquiry** An approach based on looking for what works rather than for what does not work. Appreciative inquiry challenges the traditional approach to change management in organizations, which focuses on finding problems and trying to fix them.
>
> According to Sue Annis Hammond, in *The Thin Book of Appreciative Inquiry*, "The tangible result ... describes where the organization wants to be, based on the high moments of where they have been. Because the statements are grounded in real experience and history, people know how to repeat their success."

> **Planned listening** Planned listening means proactively choosing to listen to others. It requires time, openness, and commitment on the part of the listener. It gives the listener information, enhanced understanding, and the power to act in meaningful ways. In return, planned listening fosters openness, the feeling of value, and the belief that appropriate action—including listening carefully to others—will follow in the person who's being listened to.

If you're part of a school system, your customers are administrators and support staff, parents, teachers, children, social service agencies, judicial and law enforcement agencies, colleges and universities and employers where some of your students are headed, and members of your own staff.

If you're a member of a nonprofit organization, your customers are the people who receive the dollars or services you offer. (Notice we didn't say, "who *benefit* from your dollars or services"; you won't know whether they're benefiting until you listen to them.) Your customers are the members of your board, members of the community in which you operate, donors to your cause, and volunteers for your organization.

If you're part of a for-profit organization, your customers are the people who buy your goods or services, the people who supply you with the elements of those products or the means to produce them, the people who develop your advertising and public relations, the people who live in proximity to your places of business, and the people who work in every department and division of your company.

So how does the listening start? Very simply. It starts by asking, "What do we do well?" or "What do we do right?" (Remember, you get what you ask for—and it may or may not be what you expect.) Figure 9-1 contrasts types of questions and the reactions they tend to generate.

**Smart Managing**

**The 80/20 Principle Revisited**
Remember the 80/20 principle: essentially, 80% of what you achieve derives from 20% of the time you put in. Doesn't it then make sense to ask, "What are we doing right?" and do more of it? If you expand the 20% of your really productive time to 30% or 40% or more, think what you can accomplish!

According to Hammond, in *The Thin Book of Appreciative Inquiry*, "We are obsessed with learning from our mistakes. But why not allow our successes to multiply enough to crowd out the unsuccessful? Why not follow-up with our happy customers and ask why we made them happy?"

| When You Ask This: | You Get This: |
|---|---|
| • What's wrong? | • A litany of failures. Feelings of despair, finger pointing. |
| • What's right? | • Qualities that enrich the organization. Feelings of accomplishment, energizing. |
| • Why didn't you do it this way? | • Excuses, denials, justifications. Feelings of defensiveness, holier-than-thou relationships. |
| • Why did you do it this way? or How did you decide on this approach? | • Reasons, insights. Feelings of worth, valuing. |

Figure 9-1. You get what you ask for

Take a little appreciative inquiry, add attitude, outlook, and shared vision, and—wonder of wonders!—you've effected positive change. You've begun developing a forward-looking, continuously improving, energized organization. You're on the way to creating an empowered and empowering place to work.

## Maintaining the Momentum: Valuing High Performance and Change

You can also use the appreciative inquiry approach to turn performance *appraisal* into performance *valuing*—building performance, not just dissecting it.

Back to benchmarking. Once you develop the ability to learn from your organization's history through appreciative inquiry and once you realize the necessity for shared vision, perhaps you'll look at benchmarks with a fresh perspective.

Let's look at some examples of benchmarks that you might use to transform your organization, or at least the group you manage. While we're at it, we'll ask you to think about what they might mean to your organization's performance. If you decide to make changes on the basis of benchmarks, you'll have a more appreciative eye to the possibilities inherent in such change.

### Shoot for the Moon

**Smart Managing**    In September 1962, President John F. Kennedy said that the U.S. space program would put a man on the moon and "become the world's leading space-faring nation." And he said, "We choose to go to the moon in this decade and do the other things, not because they are easy, but because they are hard, because that goal will serve to organize and measure the best of our energies and skills, because the challenge is one that we are willing to accept, one that we're unwilling to postpone, and one that we intend to win."

Don't undertake appreciative inquiry because it's easy—it won't be. It will require you to think differently, to approach others differently, and to see your organization in a different light. Undertake appreciative inquiry because it's a way to organize and measure the best of your energy and skill—and because it's the positive, empowering way to envision and manage change.

Our source for these benchmarks is the ASTD Benchmark Forum, which reported (*Training & Development*, November 1997) findings from 55 large, multinational firms, including Motorola, Corning, Intel, Texas Instruments, AT&T, Caterpillar, Bell Atlantic, and Polaroid. We'll cite just a few to give you some ideas—and raise some inquiries.

1. Work practices benchmark: 76% of the participating companies practiced job rotation or cross training. If your company adopts these approaches, what do you expect is right about them? What is it about job rotation that increases productivity? Or sparks learning? What changes do you want to see as a result of implementing cross training?

2. Employee compensation systems benchmark: 64% of the participating companies have incentive compensation systems. If your company adopts this approach to compensation, what are its advantages? What's been good about your current system of compensation? Can you keep what's good about the old while changing to the new? How will employees react to such change?

3. Performance practices benchmark: 93% of the participating companies supported attendance at conferences by their employees. If your company adds conference attendance to your professional development policies, what benefits do you anticipate? What will employees—and the organization—gain from conferences? How will it add value to the company's products or services? What will be added to organizational intelligence? How?

4. Human performance management practices benchmark: 91% of the participating companies created individual development plans for their employees. If your company initiates an individual development plan system, what benefits will accrue to each person and to the organization? How will such change enhance performance and growth? How will employees receive such a system?

When you evaluate what positive things a particular change can do for your organization (valuing) and when you have solid information about what's already right in your organization (the things you don't need to change), you'll have the makings of a plan and a vision—and of high performance. And you'll find that visionary, planned change isn't so frightening. (It's the "Who-needs-tomorrow? Just-get-me-through-the-day!" operation that's scary.)

"Remember when Jack retired last month, and we had that party for him?" Michelle asks Tom.

"Sure, I remember," Tom replies. "We had a great time reminiscing, we relived some really good times, and we laughed harder than we'd laughed in a long time."

"My point exactly," Michelle comments. "We called up memories of events we'd almost forgotten, the high spots of Jack's career—and some of the high spots of the company's history, times when we all performed our best. And it made us feel good. I'd like for us to repeat that experience more often. I'd like to remember what we did well, what made us feel good, so we can do it again."

Michelle and Tom have traveled many miles on the highway to empowerment. And they're about to pass one more milepost: they're going to ensure that their organization uses its history to develop a shared vision of the future, one that will ensure that the organization, as it moves toward empowerment, is one that's built to last. They're going to celebrate, recognizing and reinforcing the empowering culture they're helping to create.

## Manager's Checklist for Chapter 9

❑ Have a plan for change. Don't assume that another system will fit your environment or be embraced enthusiastically by your employees. Plan your own changes by adjusting benchmarks for the attitudes, skills, and goals of the people in your organization. Develop a culture of empowerment that's personalized for you and your business.

❑ If the energy in your organization results from threats or problems or maintaining the status quo or wanting more, more, more, that energy is probably short-lived. When the threat or problem dissipates, the energy dissipates along with it. When all the energy goes into maintaining the status quo, there's little left for the future. When all the energy pours into getting more, you're energizing quantity, not quality.

❑ Ask what you're doing *right*—not what you're doing *wrong*—and do more of it.

❑ Before you decide to make a change on the basis of a benchmark, turn an appreciative eye toward the benchmark and assess its value.

# Empowering for the Future: The Manager's Challenge

*It is not in the still calm of life, or in the repose of a pacific station, that great challenges are formed.... Great necessities call out great virtues.*

—Abigail Adams

Maybe you're feeling challenged enough, having made it to this point in the book. We have higher hopes for you yet, however. We'd like you to be equipped to face not only today's challenges for creating an empowered workplace but those of the future as well.

But even if we were face to face, even if we could spend days together instead of hours, we couldn't give you a prescription for the future. So what we've chosen to do is share with you a few key issues we hope will get you thinking ahead in empowering ways: technology, privacy, ethics, core values, and philanthropy.

We're sure you'll add your own insights to these issues and that you'll raise others. Just keep raising those empowering standards, and you'll be ready for anything.

## The Promise—and the Challenge—of Technology

One of those empowering standards or building blocks is *informing*, and a technology that immediately comes to mind when we talk about informing is the Internet. The Internet certainly brings promise and challenge to information sharing.

Think of the possibilities for using the Internet to reinforce empowering behaviors like information sharing, coaching, mutual influence, and continuous improvement. Here are just a few:

- Conducting training and updating information through video conferencing. What barriers such conferencing overcomes—distance, travel time and expense, the lack of face-to-face contact with email or written communications.
- Mentoring one-on-one with peers and/or with experts in a particular field, receiving immediate feedback, and breaking down geographical and cultural differences and misunderstandings.
- Saving time and frustration because you have options. Whereas "phone tag" leaves you only one choice, to leave a message for one person at a time, at one location, Internet communication offers a multitude of choices, for sender and receiver. You can transmit photos, graphics, text, sound, video—you can expand your message exponentially and meaningfully. You can reach one person in several places or several people in different places and vice versa.
- Increasing your reach and your impact. There simply are no barriers to reaching a particular audience or customer, to spreading your knowledge and your products, to sharing your knowledge and learning from others.

Perhaps the greatest promise of the Internet is that it incorporates so many of the principles of empowerment. (You'll remember some of these, we hope, from earlier chapters!) It's inclusive and democratic, it's mutually influential, it's self-directing. And it's continuously improving, growing, and broadening its scope and capabilities. All signs are that, as a result, the Internet is going to be long-lasting and resilient. It adapts to change quickly—and even embraces it.

And what about the challenges of the Internet? We've mentioned a few: using email to "hide" from direct contact or difficult conversations, for example, or managing the volume of information that the 'Net delivers.

Here's another Internet-based challenge to consider and embrace, if you're going to become part of an empowered organization. More than ever before, customers will expect personalized, customized products and services. More than ever before, you'll likely learn that from them and offer such products and services to them by way of the Internet.

So the Internet converges on one intersection along the path to empowerment. Using technology to put empowerment into practice enables you and your organization to flex, to grow, to change, to serve, to learn—not only because doing so is good for you but also because doing so prepares you for the wired future, adds value to your products and services, and develops employees who are active participants in a *kaizen* way of work.

## Balancing Privacy and Technology

There's (at least) one more challenge to empowerment that the Internet brings to mind: privacy. Although you won't find the word *privacy* in the U.S. Constitution, you probably consider it your right nevertheless. As the lines of communication expand and as the access to information grows, protecting and respecting that right becomes more and more difficult. And employees, customers, and suppliers become more and more sensitive to your approach to protecting it.

The Internet may be causing more people to become concerned now about privacy issues, but there are challenges to employee privacy throughout the workplace. Who can access personnel files and for what reasons? How secure are offices, work stations, and lockers? Privacy has long been a sensitive issue in the workplace, but the new technology of electronic mail, intranets, and the Web increases the challenge.

As an empowering manager, you'll likely be asked to take a stand on privacy issues sooner or later. Why? Because it is a sign of respect for your employees and is one more aspect of an empowered organization. "Be prepared," therefore, is probably a good motto to adopt in this case, so let's see what you can do to make that motto a reality.

Tom and Michelle have an unspoken agreement. They try to work together to anticipate issues that might arise in their workplace based on what they read or see or hear happening in other workplaces. They don't always succeed.

"I just received a memo from Human Resources," Michelle tells Tom. "A recently hired team member suspects his email is being monitored. He wants to know what company policy is and whether he can expect that his email communications are private or not."

Tom replies, "Well, I know we each have password-protected email accounts. But I don't know whether the company has a policy about privacy—and I have no idea whether someone here can access someone else's email account."

What's the issue here? If you answered "not knowing," we agree with you. (Remember the information-knowledge-wisdom continuum. You can't get to wisdom if you don't have information.) Right now, Tom and Michelle suffer from a lack of information, which means they also suffer from an inability to take appropriate action. They, like you, first need to find out what they need to know, analyze the information they find, determine whether the information is adequate, and decide how to act on their new knowledge.

Let's move farther down the road to an empowering organization as it applies to privacy and technology, then. Both are button-pushing issues today and likely to be tomorrow, as privacy laws and policies struggle to keep up with the whizzing pace of technology. You don't want this issue to undermine your efforts to empower your employees.

### Rights and Responsibilities

What do you know about rights and responsibilities in your workplace? What do you *not* know? Take a moment to answer the following questions:

- As an employer, do you have the right to know whether employees are surfing pornographic Web sites from the office computer?
- Do employees have the right to conduct personal shopping trips to Web sites during break times?
- Do you have the right to know if a prospective team member has an acquired or genetic condition that might affect your group's functioning because of lost workdays?
- Does the prospective team member have the right not to disclose that information and still be considered for the job?
- Do you have the right to use tracking devices that record where an employee is at any given moment?
- Does the employee have the right not to be photographed or otherwise tracked as long as he or she performs the job adequately?
- Do you have the right to collect and share information about your customers?
- Do your customers have the right to be notified when and how such information is used?

Most of us accept the fact that our employers may infringe on our privacy for good reason on occasion, in the interest of protecting their business interests—and therefore being able to continue to provide us with employment. But how large should the trade-off be? What's the balance between individual and organizational needs? If you want to be prepared for such questions, if you want to anticipate issues, if you want to empower employees and customers with information, you'll have to balance the needs and rights of both individuals and your organization—and you'll have to communicate clearly, completely, and in writing.

### Balancing Health Costs and Smoking

Here's an example from *The Right to Privacy* by Ellen Alderman and Caroline Kennedy. An employee of an Indiana company flunked a drug test—for nicotine. The company "forbade its employees to smoke, even on their own time at home." Ultimately, she reclaimed her job—and the legislature prohibited smoking as a firing offense. But employers now may charge smoking employees higher health insurance premiums. Privacy: it's a balancing act between right and responsibility.

Figure 10-1 raises some issues and some questions. Use it as the basis for developing your own list of privacy considerations. It's just a start, to help you raise concerns, questions, and opinions about privacy issues. We think you'll find that sharing more rather than less organizational information will create more power for you and the organization. (Think what you can do when you step outside these pages and share these issues with others in the workforce!)

### A Balanced Policy

As you're no doubt well aware, lots of legal opinions and judgments surround the issue of privacy—so many, in fact, that it's hard to keep up. But in an empowered organization, the legalities of your privacy policy may be the lesser of your concerns. Implementing empowerment means reinforcing respect, trust, and appropriate information sharing. If you respect the rights of others (both workers and customers), if you've outlined the rights of the organization, you'll have conducted a dialogue about privacy that fosters openness, awareness, and trust.

Follow these steps to develop a balanced privacy policy that's built on respect, trust, and information sharing:

1. Find out whether your organization has a privacy policy. If so, when was it last updated? Does it include technology issues?
2. Brainstorm a list of privacy issues that affect your department, team(s), customers, suppliers, and organization.
3. For each issue, develop a virtual balance scale. On the one hand, what's of concern to individual employees? To

| Privacy Considerations: Individual | Privacy Considerations: Organizational |
|---|---|
| • My email is my private communication, and no one else should have access to it. | • Does proprietary business information deserve protection, from both intentional or unintentional interception? |
| • When I make a purchase, I don't want information about me stored in a company's database. | • Does the company have legitimate need to track customers (liability, warranty, updates to products, for example)? |
| • I must be able to associate with anyone I choose. | • If that association includes sexual harassment, does the organization have the right and responsibility to know? |
| • My health habits are my own business and no one else's. | • If the company must offer its employees the best available, most reasonably priced health insurance, should it require certain health habits? |
| • I don't want my name and address given to a marketing group or to another retailer. I get enough junk mail. | • Must (or should) the organization notify customers when information about them is shared with other organizations? |
| • I don't take drugs, and I think it's an insult to be tested for them. Besides, what if the test is wrong? | • Particularly if the organization is involved in transportation or day care or medical services, for example, is the employer's potential liability high enough to warrant drug testing? |
| • Wearing a badge that tracks my movements is demeaning. If this company trusts me enough to hire me, it should trust me to move within its walls. | • What if the company's agreement with its funding sources (other corporations or government agencies, for example) requires secrecy? |
| • My sexual orientation is personal and private. My employer has no right to that information. | • If a company offers insurance to "significant others," does it have the right to information about that person, hence about the relationship? |

Figure 10-1. Privacy considerations: individual and organizational

customers? On the other hand, what's of concern to the organization as a whole?

4. Conduct a dialogue (if you've forgotten, review Chapter 6) about where the balance lies and about how policy can address the needs of the employees, the customers, and the organization. Remember that dialogue is not debate and that it doesn't necessarily result in consensus.

5. After involving all the stakeholders in a dialogue, draft a policy. Keep it simple, respectful, and honest. Then sleep on it. Have your legal department review it, if necessary, but don't let it be altered into the obscurity of legalese. Revise it as necessary and schedule it for regular review—not too often, but often enough to address changing circumstances.

6. Make sure that everyone knows the policy. It's only fair, isn't it? We can't possibly appreciate our rights—or be "response-able"—if we don't have knowledge *and* each other's support.

### Electronic Monitoring at FedEx

Does electronic monitoring add value to a company's products or services? Maybe, and maybe not, according to Ellen Alderman and Caroline Kennedy, authors of *The Right to Privacy*. Federal Express, for example, "pursued a 'people first' approach to office automation and downplayed quantitative measurements." The result? Better productivity and performance than earlier under electronic monitoring.

You'll want to be sure that your organization respects private information—and that safeguards are in place to keep the information within corporate bounds. You'll want to be sure that technology helps to *humanize* your work environment, not *demoralize it.* What is the result of such an approach? Most likely an explosion of power generated by mutual influence and shared responsibility.

## Being True: Ethics and Empowerment

This brings us to a related issue and challenge—and another milestone on the road to empowerment: *ethical behavior*. It's what more and more employees say they want to see in the organizations they work for—and it's what more and more customers want to see in the organizations they buy from.

*Fair, honest, open, reliable,* and *trustworthy* are words we might use to describe a person or a company that we see as ethical. *Moral, upstanding,* and *principled* come to mind as well.

Sometimes being ethical is easy. Sometimes right and wrong are clearly different, and it's easy for us to come down on the side of right. Sometimes right and wrong aren't so clearly defined, and taking a stand or making an ethical choice is not so easy to do.

Here's an *un*easy situation. You know one of your employees is house hunting. You also know he's likely to lose his job in your company's upcoming lay-offs. Do you warn him, tell

> **Ethical behavior** We can think of ethical behavior as being in accord with moral principles and as actions of an individual doing what's right when there is pressure to do otherwise.

him outright, or keep quiet? What are your obligations to the employee? To the company? How do you reconcile compassion with risk to the organization?

That situation is not just hypothetical. It comes from an article in *The New York Times* (Jeffrey L. Seglin, "As Layoffs Loom, Loyalties Are Divided," August 15, 1999). In this particular situation, an empowering organization holds at least one key to the resolution of this ethical dilemma. When information about the company's financial statements is openly available to employees, as it is in a growing number of companies, "an employee could probably discern for himself whether the timing was right."

Whether or not your organization has a formal code of ethics, shouldn't employee and customer alike be able to identify your core values? Are they apparent? Do you make them known? Does your own behavior reinforce them?

Remember that one of the things empowering *does* is to find the spirit in an organization and build relationships. Dialogue is an integral part of such finding and building, particularly when it's spirited dialogue: creative, constructive, and appreciative.

> ## Ethical Codes of Practice
>
> These examples illustrate how some organizations attempt to put ethical expectations on paper.
>
> "Take no personal advantage of the inexperience or lack of knowledge of our clients, customers, or our potential clients or customers."—Association of Ethical Internet Professionals' Code of Ethics, excerpt (www.aeip.com/ethics-f.html)
>
> "Engineers shall hold paramount the safety, health and welfare of the public and shall strive to comply with the principles of sustainable development in the performance of their professional duties."—American Society of Civil Engineers, Code of Ethics, Canon I (www.asce.org/membership/ethics.html)
>
> "The school develops in its students a sense of responsibility for equity and justice in the broader community."—National Association of Independent Schools, Principles of Good Practice for Member Schools, "Equity and Justice," (www.nais.org/inform/pubs/pgpequit.html)
>
> "Marketers must accept responsibility for the consequences of their activities and make every effort to ensure that their decisions, recommendations and actions function to identify, serve and satisfy all relevant publics: customers, organizations and society."—American Marketing Association, Code of Ethics, "Responsibilities of the Marketer" (www.ama.org/about/ama/fulleth.asp)

Living the ethics that are based in your organization's core values—and your own—not only conveys the company's spirit, but also builds trust among the people who create that spirit. And that which promotes more ethical behavior and more trust always contributes to an empowering environment as well.

## Sharing the Message: Family, Community, and Empowerment

Speaking of organizational spirit, we hope you realize by now that you and the other members of your organization, both individually and collectively, *are* that spirit. But the spirit of empowerment doesn't have to be confined to the walls of your office and the workplace. You may remember that empowering also *enables talent and capability* and *fosters accomplishment.* Aren't these the things you want to happen for yourself, your

> ### Patagonia: Ethics into Practice
> Patagonia, manufacturer of outdoor clothing and gear, is known for its commitment to ethical behavior and the environment. The company Web site proclaims, "We're particular about the quality and durability of the materials we use. In the process, we've learned a lot about the impact of our materials and manufacturing processes on the environment." The Web site also shows the company's commitment to environmental actions, to supporting and publicizing specific areas of activity.
>
> It's an example of ethical, honest behavior. And it's an example of empowering, sharing behavior.

family, and your community as well?

So, put your empowering business experience and knowledge to use in your life outside of work. Want to know how? (We're using our imaginations here, so we expect you to do so as well. You'll come up with your own ideas, we're sure.) Ask yourself questions like these:

- What old hobbies have you neglected? What new ones would you like to undertake?
- What new ideas or topics do you want to know more about?
- Read any good, non-work-related books lately?
- When was the last time you spent time—lots of it—talking with your spouse, your best friend, your child, and getting to know their talents and capabilities?
- Do your kids know what you value about life and work?
- Are you knowledgeable about your community? Do you know what issues affect your environment? Who's running for office and why?
- How long has it been since you shared information—including feelings—with the people you love?
- Do you set goals for your personal and community relationships and take time to think about them?

Keep in mind that empowerment isn't an isolated journey. There's no speed limit. There's an unlimited number of lanes to

### Empowerment in Life

In a televised interview following his win at the 1999 Tour de France, cyclist Lance Armstrong described how he approached his bout with testicular cancer.

He got *informed* about the disease and its treatment, from many different sources. He *learned* new skills, like reading x-rays. He *trusted* the physicians he chose. He *acted* on this information, learning, and trust.

As the interviewer remarked, "You were *empowered*" to participate in the treatment of the disease.

Empowerment's not just about corporate life. It's about life.

travel. As you grow, the highway expands to accommodate your growth—and that of others who are with you. So ask yourself how you can make that highway accessible to family, friends, and community. Then, get 'em to that on ramp!

The journey to empowerment by its very nature is meant to be shared. (That's the key to creating power.) Take every opportunity you have to share information, to mentor, to support, to provide, to transform, to create.

## Sharing the Wealth: Philanthropy and Empowerment

Here are three quotes to consider:

> Two years ago ... I attended a seminar on charitable giving and found that I could make a difference, not just with my time, but also with my money.

> Some want to take the concept of socially aware mutual funds one step further. They want to ... identify and reward companies that are setting good examples in their communities.

> What better way to gain experience than by helping a developing nation get its corporate feet on the ground?

The first quote is from a 65-year-old inner-city family practitioner who wants to ensure that others will follow him in providing medical care where it's needed (William A. Jackson, "A Gift to America's Health," *The New York Times*, August 8, 1999). He did his homework and he found a way: make a medical school that trains a large number of physicians who practice in underserved communities the beneficiary of his life insurance policies. "Making a gift of it makes me feel like a million bucks without spending a million bucks." Can you spread information about such options in your organization? How can you make your employees feel like a million bucks?

The second quote is from a market analyst for the Associated Press, in an article about investors' desire to put their retirement funds in the hands of companies that model community support and outreach (D. Prial, "Funds Will Never Be Just Right," *Pensacola News Journal*, September 15, 1999). Other investors take a slightly different approach, favoring companies that produce goods and services that are "good for us" over those whose products are less "good" or even harmful. Such investors—and maybe some of your company's employees—want to put their money where their mouths and their hearts are. Do your investors, both internal and external, see your organization as exemplary of community service?

The third quote is from a report about the "new" Peace Corps (Abby Ellin, "Joining Peace Corps Inc.," *The New York Times*, July 18, 1999). Roughly 13% of today's volunteers are placed with businesses. When asked whether they're doing a Peace Corps stint because they're altruistic or because they want their résumé to look good, the typical volunteer answers, "Both." Would your organization seek out job applicants who've made public service a part of their personal mission? Would

**Philanthropy** Altruistic concern for human beings shown through contributions to institutions that benefit society and the community. From the Greek *philos* for "loving" and *anthropos* for "human being," philanthropy means literally "loving human beings." Its meaning has been expanded to describe efforts that improve our well-being, such as charitable donations or activities that benefit others.

your company be willing to offer sabbaticals or leaves of absence for employees who want to serve?

From investing our money to investing our time, it seems that more and more of us these days want to feel as though we're giving back—or giving forward, as the case may be. Are you attuned to what employees might consider an added, if atypical, benefit of belonging to the community that is your organization? What better way to build teamwork and leadership than to coordinate efforts that make people feel good and benefit the places where they live or the causes they support?

Realize that it's not only the employees who will benefit or the community efforts that they support. Your organization will earn publicity, esteem, respect. Your products or services will have added value. Your customers will be proud—and you may attract new ones, ones who want to invest in an organization that's active in its community.

Think about it. We've talked about what workers value about jobs—and how that contributes to company loyalty. If you want to contribute to an empowered workplace, what better way than to match employees' need for philanthropy with the organization's need to be a supportive member of its community? (We call building blocks like these *serving* or *providing*, remember?)

## Back to the Future of Empowerment

What if certain individuals don't buy into the empowering principles you've learned? Within the confines of these pages, it's easy to forget that the real world doesn't always operate in black and white. So, you'll have to adapt to operating in shades of gray. You can do it, and here are a few simple suggestions (life is complicated enough!) to help you do it.

- Model empowerment as often and as consistently as you can. You'll develop your leadership skills and you'll practice following as well.
- Review the principles of empowerment every now and then. A quick refresher will help you get back on track

or help you explain your actions more effectively.

- Cut yourself some slack. You're not in this alone, remember, and that means you can't do it all by yourself. Share the wealth of information and the responsibility for empowerment.

- Tie empowering beliefs and actions to the bottom line. (This works really well for many skeptics.) What's the cost of installing adjustable keyboard trays versus the cost of harming valued employees, for example, or the cost of developing an email privacy policy versus the cost of defending a lawsuit over it?

- Perform the "Microsoft at Midnight" test. Here's how: estimate the value of your company at midnight, when the building's empty and the equipment's shut down. Pretty low, huh? The point is that it's the people who make the organization, not the other way around. If you remember that, you'll have made a giant leap forward on the highway to empowerment. Have a great trip!

## Manager's Checklist for Chapter 10

❑ Recognize the potential and the challenge of using technology in empowering ways.

❑ Get the information and participation you need to develop a privacy policy that strikes a balance between individual rights and corporate responsibility.

❑ Promote empowerment with ethical behavior that reflects your company's spirit and reinforces its core values.

❑ Put your empowering business experience and knowledge to use in your life outside of work.

❑ Consider ways in which employees can "feel like a million bucks without spending a million bucks." Total up the added value to your products and services from community involvement. Then get active!

❑ If you find that not everyone in your organization buys into empowerment, keep your sanity with a few simple actions: model empowering behavior and attitudes, review empowering principles, cut yourself some slack, tie empowering activities to the bottom line, and perform the "Microsoft at Midnight" test.

# An Empowering Journey

*The beginnings and endings of all human undertakings are untidy, the building of a house, the writing of a novel, the demolition of a bridge, and eminently, the finish of a voyage.*
　　　　　—John Galsworthy, *Over the River*

The room's quiet. The feeling's relaxed, almost peaceful. Yet there's strong energy emanating from the room's two occupants.

Michelle faces Tom across a conference table, in the room where they've now met many times—alone, with their project teams, or with various ad hoc groups.

"It seems like such a short time ago," Michelle says, "that we didn't have a clue about what empowerment really means."

Tom nods in agreement. "And I can remember when I thought empowerment was just overused, consultant-coined, program-of-the-month jargon," he adds. "Now, when I think how we've changed, how far we've come, and how much we've learned, I'm astounded."

"The only thing that astounds me more than how far we've come is how far we can go!" Michelle exclaims. "When we started, I didn't really trust in the one-plus-one-equals-more-than-two concept of power. Now, you can't convince me that one-plus-one equals anything but infinite creative power and possibilities."

Tom's eager to jump back into the conversation. "It hasn't always been easy—and I expect we'll find a few potholes in the road to empowerment—but it's been worth every effort.

"I remember thinking at first that empowering was something that was being done *to* me or *for* me, but it hasn't been that kind of experience at all. Once I realized how information and interaction—mutual influence—worked to increase our team's knowledge and power, I realized that empowering is something you do *with* others."

"While we're taking a stroll down memory lane," Michelle adds, "I remember thinking that I already knew how to manage, that I could do the basics in my sleep: planning, decision making, leading, informing, mentoring, organizing.

"What a revelation to find out there's more, a higher level— or levels—of learning, transforming, liberating, coaching, serving, creating, and beyond. And to find that we can achieve them together."

Tom thinks for a moment. "When you said 'together,' it made me realize that we've talked an awful lot about how moving toward empowerment has affected us—but we've been anything but alone in this process. It's had an amazing impact on everyone else in the organization.

"We've seen people who mistrusted each other learn to open up and stop hoarding secrets—and then we've seen them realize that the power lies in joint effort, not in heroics. We've seen folks who'd never uttered a word in a meeting begin to develop skills that make them capable of leading a meeting when their leadership is needed. We've witnessed people, frustrated by a 'nowhere to go but *up*' hierarchy, become much happier moving *across* a flatter organization. We've seen people expand their skills and develop new ones, and we've found resources we never dreamed of, ones that have made our work lives much more fulfilling and rewarding."

"Let's not forget our customers," Michelle points out. "That last survey indicated a considerable change in their confidence and satisfaction. The more open and communicative we become, the more they seem to do the same."

Tom starts to laugh. "I never thought I'd say it, but I'm feeling empowered—and looking forward to becoming more so."

An experience like Michelle's and Tom's is nothing less than what we wish for you: wisdom, freedom, appreciation, transformation.

The journey to empowerment is never finished. And you won't want it to be.

# The Management Styles Survey: A Manager's Perception

*We know what we are, but know not what we may be.*
—William Shakespeare, *Hamlet*

Now that you know some characteristics of empowering, we'd like you to know some characteristics of your own. This appendix offers you a tool to do just that: The Management Styles Survey: A Manager's Perception. You won't be alone. Since 1992, more than 10,000 managers have used the survey to understand themselves better—and to pinpoint where they fit on a continuum of empowering beliefs and behaviors.

Then again, you will be alone. We won't be there to look over your shoulder, and we'll never know whether you use the survey or not. So, before you're tempted to close the book, we'd like to tell you why we think you should answer the survey questions.

First, the survey questions are grounded in a study that began more than 25 years ago, a study of global perspectives on management competencies. At the time, there were two

positions on the subject. One held that there are universal principles of management and that management according to those
principles will be good anywhere in the world. The other position held that each company, country, or environment is unique
and that universal principles therefore did not apply.

This survey finds a place between the two positions, creating a matrix of six core management competencies (informing,
decision making, evaluating, motivating, planning, and developing) and six assumptions about empowering management (the
second-generation empowering competencies from Chapter 2).

> **CAUTION!**
>
> **A Survey,
> Not a Test**
>
> The Management Styles
> Survey is not a test or an evaluation or
> a performance measure. You'll derive
> the most value from it if you view it as
> a way to think about which behaviors
> and views you'd like to change—and
> which you're satisfied with.
>
> Think of the survey as a way to
> start a conversation with yourself, not
> as a way to find out whether you
> "measure up."

What that means is that
the survey accounts for
both universal principles
and cultural factors. It
means that when you fin-
ish the survey, you will
know more about what
you are now and what you
may be in the future, on a
management continuum of
best common practices
and adaptive, unique
behaviors.

## The Management Styles Survey: A Manager's Perception

This survey is for you. You will answer the questions, you will
score the results, you will analyze what the results mean, and
you will decide how to use the results to move along the
empowering continuum.

### Your Mindset

So, be as candid as you can. Treat each item individually. Don't
try to ferret out relationships among items. Just try to answer
objectively about your own behavior. If you do so, the survey will
more clearly identify your management style—and give you

insights into how you can become a more empowering manager.

## The Instructions

For each item, you'll find a lead-in statement, a five-point continuum of response choices, and two endpoint statements. Here's an example:

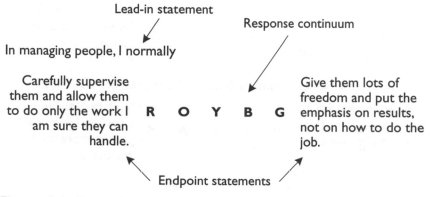

Figure A-1. Example of a survey item

When you're ready to complete the survey, follow this procedure:

1. Read the lead-in statement.
2. Read each endpoint statement.
3. Circle the letter along the five-point response continuum that best corresponds to your behavior. Circle the midpoint, for example, if you behave equally as often at either endpoint. (The letters used for the five points along the response continuum vary from item to item. Don't be distracted; we'll explain that part in the section on scoring.)

I. When communicating with my subordinates, I normally

| Provide only the information that is absolutely needed to do the job. | R O Y B G | Provide more information than is needed and try to help them understand the larger picture. |

2. If I could build the perfect information system, it would

Give as many people as possible access to nonconfidential information.　**N　U　L　A　E**　Provide others with only the information they need to get their jobs done.

3. When discussing my job with coworkers, I try to

Reveal only what I think they have a right to know.　**R　O　Y　B　G**　Discuss my work freely—perhaps they can assist me or I can help them.

4. When I communicate with my boss or those in higher positions, I am

Eager to explain what I know and what I think about any subject that seems important.　**N　U　L　A　E**　Very cautious of what I say lest I give the wrong impression or say too much.

5. When communicating information, I usually

Do whatever I can to ensure that information goes where it is needed to get the job done.　**G　B　Y　O　R**　Make sure information is needed before passing it along.

6. When I make a decision and take action, I am

Usually in agreement with the others concerned; I see my actions as part of a larger whole.　**N　U　L　A　E**　The sole person responsible; I exert my power as necessary.

7. When I am pressured for a fast decision, I

Immediately make a decision and take responsibility for it.　**R　O　Y　B　G**　Quickly size up the situation, determine whether anyone else needs to be involved, and if so, delay making a decision.

8. When it comes to action, I am firmly convinced that

The power of the group to decide and act should prevail if the conditions are right and the group is well developed.     **N   U   L   A   E**     An individual can get much more done more quickly than any group.

9. When my boss delegates a job to me, I will usually

Take full responsibility and get the job done by myself whenever possible.     **R   O   Y   B   G**     Work with others to get the job done and to ensure and share success.

10. I encourage my subordinates to

Work as a team; teams are more powerful than people working alone and are able to do more without my help.     **N   U   L   A   E**     Work alone and report to me because I will take care of them.

11. When I plan, I prefer to

Do it myself first, then show my boss, then tell my subordinates what to expect.     **R   O   Y   B   G**     Work with others to develop a larger plan first, then share the planning activity with my subordinates.

12. When I organize my work and my subordinates, I

Carefully explain the larger picture and then work with the groups involved to define their responsibilities.     **N   U   L   A   E**     Clearly describe each person's job, responsibilities, and reporting structure.

13. To get a work project accomplished, it is best to

Tell employees exactly what to do one step at a time, then tell them how much time they have to complete each step.     **R   O   Y   B   G**     Coordinate the total project first, then go back over each step so that everyone knows what is required and how his or her work fits into the project as a whole.

14. When a work project is very complicated and involved, my manager prefers to

Work with a team to ensure that all the pieces fit together and that everyone knows what everyone else is doing.

**N    U    L    A    E**

Take complete charge and simplify each part so that the project is manageable, rather than depending on people's ability to work together.

15. The best way to design an organization is to

Centralize power and authority so that all employees are informed about managerial decisions and organizational happenings.

**R    O    Y    B    G**

Encourage delegation of authority and power sharing as much as possible in order to use all employees to their capacities.

16. When I evaluate my subordinates, I usually

Share my evaluations and give subordinates a chance to respond.

**N    U    L    A    E**

Fill out the proper forms and send a copy to Personnel but try not to make a big deal of it.

17. The people who work for me always know

I am the boss, and my evaluations of their performance will determine such things as raises and promotions.

**R    O    Y    B    G**

How they are doing, in what areas they are doing well, and in what areas they need improvement.

18. My approach to control is to

Help subordinates build self-control and achieve higher levels of responsibility in the organization.

**N    U    L    A    E**

Keep a careful eye on all that goes on and be sure there is a developed system of controls.

19. The best way to ensure that work is done on time is to

Set specific deadlines, constantly monitor progress, and discipline those who are late.

**R O Y B G**

Be sure everyone understands the deadlines and how they affect others' work; reward and recognize timely performance.

20. When an employee needs to be disciplined, I try to

Discuss the problem, look for longer-term solutions before consequences are determined, and document the infraction.

**N U L A E**

Make sure the punishment fits the "crime" and let everyone know what happens to problem employees.

21. As a leader, I always try to

Be out in front of my people, know more about their jobs than they do in order to preserve my leadership status.

**R O Y B G**

Inspire others, set an example, and work collaboratively with others.

22. To motivate employees, I

Look for the kind of work and the setting in which they can best perform.

**N U L A E**

Reward and punish them as I deem appropriate.

23. In my experience, I have found that subordinates are most motivated by

More money, more time off, and more status.

**R O Y B G**

Recognition and satisfaction resulting from doing a good job.

24. In leadership, it is most important to

Work with people in such a way that they become more powerful and successful.

**N U L A E**

Always show that you know where you are going and have strength and confidence in your own opinions.

25. When I work with unmotivated employees, I usually

Try to figure out what it will take to make them work and watch them closely to keep them moving.    **R    O    Y    B    G**    Work with them to get to know them better, then help them find the work best suited to their abilities or help them find another job.

26. When selecting new employees, I

Try to match the job to the person to facilitate long-term success.    **N    U    L    A    E**    Try to screen out troublemakers, lazy people, and those I could not manage well.

27. When a subordinate does not perform a job well, I usually

Counsel that person and, if that does not work, look for a replacement before firing that person.    **R    O    Y    B    G**    Sit down with the person and try to determine what it will take to get the job done well.

28. When working with people, I try to act as if

Employees can always achieve more; together we can make any situation better; we can learn from working together.    **N    U    L    A    E**    Employees will be rewarded when they do as they are told; if they do not, they will be disciplined.

29. If I have worked with someone for several years, I

Believe he or she should know the boundaries of the job and what I expect.    **R    O    Y    B    G**    Should be able to see how he or she has grown in the job and become more valuable to the organization.

30. If someone is not growing in his or her job, I usually

Try to understand the problem and do whatever I can to help.    **N    U    L    A    E**    Believe there are no problems as long as the person still gets the work done and works well with his or her boss.

## Your Score

Scoring your survey involves four steps:

1. Calculate a score for each of six areas and total the six scores.
2. Plot your area scores along the six continua.
3. Plot your total score.
4. Interpret your scores.

## Calculate Your Area Scores and Your Grand Total

When you score your survey, you'll first work in six areas: information and communication, decision making and action, planning and organizing, evaluating and control, leadership and motivation, and selection, placement, and development.

For each area:

1. Add the number of responses for O's and A's and multiply by 2.
2. Add the Y's and L's and multiply by 5.
3. Add the B's and U's and multiply by 8.
4. Add the G's and N's and multiply by 10.
5. Total the four calculations to arrive at the area total.

Repeat steps 1-5 for all six areas.

Total all area totals to arrive at a grand total. (Note: R's and E's have a value of zero, so you don't need to include them in your score.)

Figure A-2 shows an example scoring sheet for one area.

| Area | Number of Responses | Multiply By | Response Total | Area Total |
|---|---|---|---|---|
| 1. Informing Items 1-5 | O and A __1__ <br> Y and L __2__ <br> B and U __1__ <br> G and N __1__ | x2 <br> x5 <br> x8 <br> x10 | __2__ <br> __10__ <br> __8__ <br> __10__ | Area 1 <br><br> __30__ |

Figure A-2. Example scoring by area

Here's where you get to score your survey. Use the scoring sheet in Figure A-3.

| Area | Number of Responses | Multiply By | Response Total | Area Total |
|---|---|---|---|---|
| 1. Informing<br>Items 1-5 | O and A ___<br>Y and L ___<br>B and U ___<br>G and N ___ | x2<br>x5<br>x8<br>x10 | ___<br>___<br>___<br>___ | Area 1<br><br><br>___ |
| 2. Decision<br>Making<br>Items 6-10 | O and A ___<br>Y and L ___<br>B and U ___<br>G and N ___ | x2<br>x5<br>x8<br>x10 | ___<br>___<br>___<br>___ | Area 2<br><br><br>___ |
| 3. Planning<br>Items 11-15 | O and A ___<br>Y and L ___<br>B and U ___<br>G and N ___ | x2<br>x5<br>x8<br>x10 | ___<br>___<br>___<br>___ | Area 3<br><br><br>___ |
| 4. Evaluating<br>Items 16-20 | O and A ___<br>Y and L ___<br>B and U ___<br>G and N ___ | x2<br>x5<br>x8<br>x10 | ___<br>___<br>___<br>___ | Area 4<br><br><br>___ |
| 5. Motivating<br>Items 21-25 | O and A ___<br>Y and L ___<br>B and U ___<br>G and N ___ | x2<br>x5<br>x8<br>x10 | ___<br>___<br>___<br>___ | Area 5<br><br><br>___ |
| 6. Developing<br>Items 26-30 | O and A ___<br>Y and L ___<br>B and U ___<br>G and N ___ | x2<br>x5<br>x8<br>x10 | ___<br>___<br>___<br>___ | Area 6<br><br><br>___ |

Figure A-3. Your survey scores (area totals and grand total)

## Plot Your Area Scores

In Figure A-4, each area is represented by a continuum. Place an "x" at the spot along the line for each area that corresponds to your score in that area. For example, if your Area 1 score is

36, put an "x" on the Area 1 line halfway between the numbers 29 and 42.

**Area I**
**Informing**                                                          **Learning**

0              7              20             29             42            50

| | | | | |

**Area 2**
**Decision Making**                                              **Transforming**

0              7              20             29             42            50

| | | | | |

**Area 3**
**Planning**                                                            **Serving**

0              7              20             29             42            50

| | | | | |

**Area 4**
**Evaluating**                                                        **Liberating**

0              7              20             29             42            50

| | | | | |

**Area 5**
**Motivating**                                                        **Coaching**

0              7              20             29             42            50

| | | | | |

**Area 6**
**Developing**                                                        **Creating**

0              7              20             29             42            50

| | | | | |

Figure A-4. Your plot of area scores

## Plot Your Grand Total Score

Plot your grand total score on the diagram in Figure A-5. Put an "x" on the top line closest to where your total score falls. For example, if your grand total is 65, put an "x" on the line about one-quarter of the way between the numbers 45 and 125.

**Grand Total**

| Basic Competencies | | | | Empowering Competencies | |
|---|---|---|---|---|---|
| 0 | 45 | 125 | 175 | 255 | 300 |

Figure A-5. Your plot of grand total score

## Interpret Your Scores

Now that you've calculated and plotted your scores, you've also identified empowering behavior that we hope will give you some personal insight. Use the interpretations in Figure A-6 in two ways:

1. to interpret your scores in each of the six areas and
2. to interpret your grand total score.

# What's Ahead

Earlier in this book, we explored what empowering is and what it does. And now we've discovered where you are along the continuum of empowering behaviors.

As you journey toward empowerment, you'll find that you move from a position of control to one of greater and greater flexibility.

We've shared tips and cautions, procedures and how-to's, definitions and examples. You'll be able to personalize them now, based on your own empowering qualities.

| Scores | Style | Interpretation |
|---|---|---|
| Area: 0-7<br>Grand Total:<br>0-45 | Personalized power extreme | The least-empowering management style. Tightly controls power in the organization. Very concerned with control and power. Takes on all responsibility. |
| Area: 8-20<br>Grand Total:<br>46-125 | Controlling | Very limited empowering style. Not oriented toward mutual influence. Seldom shares, creates, or empowers subordinates. |
| Area: 21-29<br>Grand Total:<br>126-174 | Middle of the road | Combines controlling and empowering in somewhat equal proportions. Rarely acts in the extreme when it comes to the use of power. |
| Area: 30-42<br>Grand Total:<br>175-254 | Empowering | More empowering than controlling. Helps move the organization toward empowerment. |
| Area: 43-50<br>Grand Total:<br>255-300 | Socialized power extreme | Most empowering style. Not only shares power but also creates it. Is very open to mutual influence and shared responsibility. |

Figure A-6. Interpreting your scores

# Index